*The Story of the Word*

# The Story of the Word

Meditations on the Narrative of Scripture

Trevor Laurence

WIPF & STOCK · Eugene, Oregon

THE STORY OF THE WORD
Mediations on the Narrative of Scripture

Copyright © 2017 Trevor Laurence. All rights reserved. Except for brief quotations in critical publications or reviews, no part of this book may be reproduced in any manner without prior written permission from the publisher. Write: Permissions, Wipf and Stock Publishers, 199 W. 8th Ave., Suite 3, Eugene, OR 97401.

Wipf & Stock
An Imprint of Wipf and Stock Publishers
199 W. 8th Ave., Suite 3
Eugene, OR 97401

www.wipfandstock.com

PAPERBACK ISBN: 978-1-5326-1166-7
HARDCOVER ISBN: 978-1-5326-1168-1
EBOOK ISBN: 978-1-5326-1167-4

Manufactured in the U.S.A.                JANUARY 6, 2017

Scripture quotations are from the ESV® Bible (The Holy Bible, English Standard Version®), copyright © 2001 by Crossway, a publishing ministry of Good News Publishers. Used by permission. All rights reserved.

To Tiernan,
May the Lord grow you in love
for his word and the Christ to whom it testifies.

# Contents

*Acknowledgments | ix*
*Introduction | xi*

Part One: From Creation to Christ

    1    The Beginning of All Things | 3
    2    In the Garden of the Lord | 6
    3    The Fall of Man | 9
    4    The Flood of Judgment | 13
    5    God's Covenant with Abram | 17
    6    The Sacrifice of Isaac | 21
    7    Slavery and the Promise of Rescue | 24
    8    The Passover and Exodus | 28
    9    The Ten Commandments | 31
    10    Blessings, Curses, and Forgiveness | 35
    11    The Covenant with David | 38
    12    The Temple of God | 41
    13    A Baby and a Branch | 44
    14    The Suffering Servant of the Lord | 48
    15    The New Covenant | 52

Part Two: From the Manger to the (Empty) Tomb

    16    The Birth of the King | 59
    17    The Water and the Wilderness | 62
    18    The Ministry of Jesus | 65
    19    A Blessing and a Prayer | 69

| | | |
|---|---|---|
| 20 | The Night Meeting | 73 |
| 21 | The Bread of Life | 77 |
| 22 | The Arrival of the King | 81 |
| 23 | A New Command | 84 |
| 24 | The Father, The Spirit, and the Son | 88 |
| 25 | The High Priestly Prayer | 92 |
| 26 | The Table of the Lord | 96 |
| 27 | In the Garden of Anguish | 100 |
| 28 | The Court of Injustice | 104 |
| 29 | The Cross | 108 |
| 30 | The Empty Tomb | 112 |

Interlude | 116

Part Three: From Christ's Ascension to Christ's Return

| | | |
|---|---|---|
| 31 | The Commission | 123 |
| 32 | The Ascension of the King | 127 |
| 33 | The Sending of the Spirit | 131 |
| 34 | Righteous by Faith | 135 |
| 35 | More Than Conquerors | 139 |
| 36 | Living Sacrifices | 143 |
| 37 | The Foolishness of God | 147 |
| 38 | By Faith or by Works? | 151 |
| 39 | Walk by the Spirit | 155 |
| 40 | The Riches of Grace | 159 |
| 41 | To Live Is Christ, To Die Is Gain | 163 |
| 42 | A Pilgrim Faith | 167 |
| 43 | The Throne and the Lamb | 171 |
| 44 | The Thousand Years | 175 |
| 45 | The End of All Things | 179 |

# Acknowledgments

A PROJECT LIKE THIS is, in one sense, years in the making. In another sense, it's the product of a whole lifetime, and there have been many who contributed to what lies in these pages in ways large and small.

Mom and Dad, thank you for passing on a love for Scripture and teaching me that the only way to understand the word of the King is to first humbly submit to his loving reign. And Mom, your willingness to read through this entire book with a mother's love and an English teacher's eye has undoubtedly made the finished product more readable and helpful than it otherwise would have been.

Derek Radney, your friendship was God's gracious way of introducing me to the Jesus-saturated story of the Bible. Thank you for reading the first drafts of each meditation and offering your insights. Thank you more for your commitment to me as a brother in the Lord.

Sandeep and Gretchen Mazumder, thank you for your consistent encouragements during the writing process. You blessed me on a weekly basis as you made an effort to tell me how these meditations were opening up the Scriptures for you and making your hearts sing.

And to Sylvia, thank you for making a promise to me, to love me and walk beside me in repentance and faith as we both follow after Jesus. So much of this book grew from the seeds of your everyday ministry to me: conversations over dinner, comfort in pain, gracious exhortations toward holiness. You push me to live more faithfully as a character in God's story of the world. I love you, dear one.

# Introduction

"But as for you, continue in what you have learned and have firmly believed, knowing from whom you learned it and how from childhood you have been acquainted with the sacred writings, which are able to make you wise for salvation through faith in Christ Jesus. All Scripture is breathed out by God and profitable for teaching, for reproof, for correction, and for training in righteousness, that the man of God may be complete, equipped for every good work."[1] So wrote the apostle Paul to his dear brother Timothy. Scripture is a precious gift from the triune God to his people and is to be treasured, read, prayed over, proclaimed, studied, discussed, applied, and celebrated in song. As a pastor of a local church, this passage summarizes my desire for myself, my family, and the sheep under my care. With Paul's words before us, let me share a few of my reasons for writing this little book.

*First, this book is intended to encourage you to make use of Scripture as a means of grace.* God promises to meet with and speak to his children through his word. In Scripture we hear about God's creating and redeeming work in the world. We hear his sweet promises to us in the gospel of Jesus—the good news of his life, death, and resurrection for the forgiveness of sin. We hear about his law and his desire for his children to glorify him by trusting and obeying his word. The Holy Spirit ministers the word of Scripture to our hearts, confirming its truth, convicting of sin, comforting with the gospel, and shaping our character as we hear and believe all that God has said and done. It's ironic, then, how easy it can be to neglect this treasure. My hope is that this book will help Christians go to the word to hear from and learn to love the God who reveals himself there.

---

1. 2 Tim 3:14–16.

## Introduction

*Second, this book is intended to familiarize you with the whole story of the Bible.* Many of us tend to approach the Bible as if it's a collection of moral stories or a disjointed series of spiritual episodes. But it is far more! In Scripture we have God's story of the whole world—from creation to completion. The Bible gives us a single, unified narrative that traces God's covenant faithfulness and saving work from the beginning in Eden to the end in the new heavens and new earth, a story that centers on Jesus Christ and his fulfillment of all God's promises. A lot of Christians can quote a handful of Bible verses. Some can even describe the major events of the Old and New Testaments. But far fewer can trace the connectedness and significance of God's story throughout the Scriptures. This book offers meditations on many of the texts that shape the plot of the Bible's narrative and can therefore help you to see the profound unity and beauty of the story of God's word.

*Third, this book is intended to teach you how to begin interpreting Scripture.* Often, our approach to interpreting the Bible includes little more than looking for an example of what to do or not do and then applying that principle to our situations. But if Scripture is in fact a unified story that finds its ultimate meaning in the life, death, and resurrection of Jesus Christ, then in order to correctly interpret the Bible, we have to understand how to read it through the lens of the gospel. As we look at Scripture together and explore how God's story culminates in Jesus, I hope you'll be equipped to read, understand, and apply God's word in a way that recognizes Christ's centrality and supremacy.

*Fourth, this book is intended to bring the story of God to bear on your whole life.* Each of us has our own story, and we tend to live as if we're the writers, directors, and main characters. This posture, however, misses the *true* writer, director, and main character of our lives—and with destructive consequences. Yes, each of us has a story, but our individual stories are part of the grand story of what God is doing in the world, the story that he tells us in Scripture. As we grow to love and understand God's story, we'll also learn the meaning of life—our purpose, our role, how we're to participate as creatures in God's world for our flourishing and the glory of his name. My prayer is that God's narrative in the Bible would form us to walk faithfully as his people in every sphere of life.

This book consists of forty-five meditations on Scripture that cover many of the most significant passages in the plot line of God's story. I've organized the meditations into three groups of fifteen that move from

# Introduction

creation to Christ, from the manger to the (empty) tomb, and from Christ's ascension to Christ's return.

You can use this devotional guide in a couple ways. If you work through one meditation every weekday, you'll journey through the Bible's story in nine weeks. Or you could spend a whole week studying each selected passage—soaking it in, as it were—and traverse Scripture's narrative in a little less than a year.

Each selection begins with a Scripture citation that directs you to a passage to read from the Bible. What follows is a short meditation that seeks to bring out the major themes in the text and connect the passage to the larger story of Scripture. At the end of each meditation, I've included a brief prayer to prompt your response to God as you continue to commune with him by speaking to him and enjoying all the glories of his character and work.

The love of God the Father, the grace of the Lord Jesus Christ, and the fellowship of the Holy Spirit be with you now and always. To God be the glory. Amen.

# Part One

## From Creation to Christ

# 1

# The Beginning of All Things

## Genesis 1:1—2:3

THE BIBLE BEGINS WITH the Trinity—the Father, the Son, and the Spirit, existing in perfect love and fellowship and together bringing the whole cosmos into existence. God the Father speaks, "Let there be." God the Son, himself the Word and Wisdom of the Father, goes forth as the one through whom all things are made, the mediator of the Father's creative work.[1] God the Spirit hovers over the face of the waters, preparing to animate and give life to the world.

God's creation begins "without form and void."[2] It's uncrafted and empty, but it won't stay that way. In the first three days, God forms his creation into realms and habitations, giving structure and order to his universe and his world. In days four through six, he fills those realms, setting up rulers who will occupy those habitations and exercise dominion in them.

The supreme creative act, however, takes place when God makes humanity in his own image and likeness. God is the ultimate King who exercises authority over all things, and when he creates man and woman in his image, he commissions them to reflect his kingship by ruling over, cultivating, and filling his world in submission to his word. Humans aren't given permission to function as authoritarian monarchs or autonomous dictators. We're made in God's image to exercise kingship in covenant with the King of kings as we worship, trust, and obey the one true Lord.

---

1. See Prov 8:22–31; John 1:1–3; Col 1:15–17.
2. Gen 1:2.

When God rests on the seventh day, he does so as the sovereign King whose reign knows no boundary. Everything that he created exists because of him, under him, and for him. God rests on the Sabbath day, enthroned in glory over his creation. He has crafted a world where he can dwell in holiness and love with his creation, where he can bless his people with the glory of his presence. In other words, this introduction to the book of Genesis tells us that God the King has lovingly constructed his world as a palace—a temple—where Creator and creature can live together in covenant joy.

Genesis 1:1—2:3 is the first act of God's story—his drama of redemption—and it establishes themes that will be built upon and expanded throughout the whole Bible. Let's consider four.

## God's Sovereign Holiness

The creation narratives of other ancient cultures often depicted the world emerging from a cosmic war between multiple gods vying with one another for supremacy. But the Genesis account emphasizes that God alone creates all things by the power of his word. He doesn't entertain competitors or rivals, and nothing exists alongside him that can impinge upon his claim to be the holy and sovereign Lord. God created the universe *ex nihilo* (from nothing), demonstrating that he's the King over all things, gloriously set apart from all creation as the Creator. Contrary to the modern notion that the observable, physical world is all that exists, the Bible is clear that there is indeed a God who stands outside of the natural world as the compassionate giver of life.

## Creation's Purpose

Everything in the Genesis account leads up to God's Sabbath enthronement and enjoyment of his creation. All that was made in the six days of creation is consecrated, devoted, and placed in submission to God. The heavens and earth, the sun and stars, the plants and animals, and you and I were created for the glory of the Lord—to magnify his beauty, delight in his character, and find our greatest joy in worshiping him through all of life.

The Beginning of All Things

## Humanity in God's image

Man and woman were made in God's image to exist in covenant with their Lord. This means that every human being possesses a profound dignity as one who belongs to and was made for God, and this understanding of humanity is one of the central reasons why we're called to love, honor, and respect all people out of love for God. But this also means that we're made to enjoy God in covenant as we worship and submit to him. To live in the image of God is to magnify the glory of the Lord by imitating and obeying God in faith and worship. As the rest of the Bible's story makes clear, humanity has rebelled against God and has created lesser gods to worship and obey, but the fact remains that we are worshiping creatures. We're creatures who have an undeniable religious impulse, who are always worshiping something or someone, because our Creator made us for himself. Only when Jesus arrives as the truly faithful image of God to fulfill the obligations of our covenant can sinners be restored to fellowship with God and progressively renewed in his image.[3]

## God with us

It's clear from our passage that God is no disinterested Creator. Rather, as a God who crafts the world to be his temple—his dwelling place—and who makes human beings to know him in covenant fellowship, God demonstrates that his desire from the beginning has been to welcome his creatures into the joyous life of the triune Father, Son, and Holy Spirit. Not even the treason of sin could inhibit God's purpose to dwell with his people, for Jesus Christ, our great Immanuel, was sent to be God with us so that we might spend an eternity with him, delighting in the glory of the Lord.

So begins the story of the word, the story of God's purposes in the world, the story of us all.

*Holy God, your works are wondrous, your ways are wise, and your character is glorious. Help us to recognize your holiness, submit to your sovereign kingship, and live into the purpose for which we were made. In Christ Jesus, you deal with our rebellion and invite us back into the joy of your presence. As we trust his work for us, grow us into your image, that we may reflect your glorious beauty in faithful obedience and enjoy the blessings of life in covenant with you.*

3. Col 1:15; 3:9–10.

# 2

# In the Garden of the Lord
## *Genesis 2:4–25*

GENESIS 1 PROVIDED A cosmic perspective on God's creation of the world. Genesis 2 offers a complementary account of God's creative activity, focusing the universal vision of the Bible's first chapter squarely on human beings and their formation and place in God's world. *Who are we?* is one of the fundamental questions that every philosophy, religion, and story of the world has to answer. The Christian answer to the question of human identity and significance which began in Genesis 1 is now filled out even more in this passage.

In ancient pagan mythologies, human beings were often conceived of as savage servants whose sole purpose was to make life easier for the gods. But this low view of humanity isn't just a relic of a superstitious past. The common modern perspective says that humans are merely complex biological organisms—separated from other animals only in terms of intellectual and behavioral sophistication—who must create their own meaning in life. Ironically, while the modern view exalts human independence and self-determination by rejecting any authority to which we must submit, it at the same time devalues humanity with the claim that there's no inherent dignity in purely physical human beings.

Yet in the Bible, humans are the special and beloved creations of God, made in his very image to live in covenant communion with the maker of all things. Adam, the first man, is only a creature—formed from the dust of the ground—but a creature for whom the Lord demonstrates a unique care and concern as God himself breathes into Adam's nostrils the breath of life. Humanity is called to serve the Lord, but as a son and not as a slave—as one who finds his utmost joy in imitating the Lord of glory and fulfilling his commands in thankful worship. The significance of human beings in God's creative design is clear, especially when compared to alternative visions of humanity. Moderns exalt human autonomy while stripping human dignity, but the Bible reverses this in a beautiful way, showing us that human beings are tremendously precious as image bearers of God and are made to find meaning, satisfaction, and life in submission to the one, true King. That single truth has the power to make you more compassionately generous in your estimation of others, more securely humble in your estimation of yourself, and more gladly devoted in your estimation of God than any other philosophy, religion, or vision of life.

God instructs Adam to work and keep the garden, a job description that shows up again when God commissions the priestly Levites to serve the Lord and guard the tabernacle. What might that mean? It means that Adam was created not merely to cultivate the earth, but to serve as a holy priest who cares for and guards the garden-temple where the Lord resides with his people. But Adam is made to function as a prophet as well. He receives the word of the Lord and is responsible for spreading the knowledge of God as he and his family multiply over the face of the earth. So Adam is a *king*, an image bearer called to subdue the earth and exercise dominion in covenant with God. He's a *priest* charged with serving faithfully in the presence of the Lord. And he's a *prophet* commissioned to receive and communicate God's word in the world.

It's clear, however, that Adam isn't intended to live independently. He's made for the relationships of community—community with God and with others. The Lord declares that it's not good for man to be alone and elects to fashion a helper for him. None of the animals will do, so God forms Eve from Adam's rib and presents her to her husband in the first ever marriage ceremony—a heavenly Father leading the bride to her groom. And just as man and woman were made from the one flesh of Adam, husbands and wives are to join again in the one flesh union of marriage, uniting their bodies and their entire lives into a single whole. The implications of this text for a Christian view of the world are enormous. Christian beliefs about community, marriage, family, sexuality, and gender are all rooted in the narrative of God's creation.

In the garden, God plants two special trees. The Lord commands Adam not to eat of the tree of the knowledge of good and evil, and in so doing the covenant making God places limits on his creatures. Humanity is

## Part One: From Creation to Christ

to live under the authoritative word of the Lord, not according to whatever he decides for himself. This tree of knowledge stands in the garden as a sign that man is not autonomous but dependent upon God's revelation. And the curse for breaking covenant with God is death.

Also present in the garden is the tree of life. This is no magical tree. Rather, it's a sign and seal of God's covenant with Adam. The tree symbolizes that if Adam obeys the Lord and walks in covenant obedience, life with God is his. Eating of the tree would thus seal and confirm that Adam had entered the Sabbath rest of God to enjoy the glory of the Lord forever.

Taken together, these two trees emphatically hang a question over the Bible's story: Will Adam obey God, fulfill his purpose in covenant with the Lord, and enter God's Sabbath joy with all the blessings of life? Of course, the answer of Genesis 3 is *no, he won't*. Rather than walking in covenant faithfulness and enjoying the covenant blessings, Adam and Eve will break covenant with God and merit the curse of death. And the rest of the Bible's story will follow God's gracious, redemptive work to deal with sin and death and welcome his people into his Sabbath rest in spite of what they deserve. Adam will fail as a representative of the human race—as prophet, priest, and king—and the results will be devastating. So as we consider God's creation of humanity, we're left hoping for one who will succeed in keeping God's covenant and usher us into life with God.

*Covenant God, we confess that too often we treat our neighbors—your image bearers—as if they're disposable and insignificant, and we think of ourselves as if we're our own gods. As we hear in your word that humanity is made for covenant with you, we recognize our wickedness and folly. Shape us according to your word that we might live according to your purposes. And lift our hearts to trust in the only one who was able to keep covenant with you, the Lord Jesus Christ, who shares with his people the blessings of life and welcomes us into the glory of your Sabbath rest.*

# 3

# The Fall of Man
## *Genesis 3*

ADAM AND EVE, as priests in God's garden-temple, were charged with cultivating and guarding the place of God's presence as they multiplied and extended God-glorifying human society over the face of the earth. When confronted with the crafty serpent—whom Revelation 12:9 explicitly identifies with Satan himself—the only proper response would be to expel him from Eden, but Adam and Eve instead tolerate his presence, give ear to his deception, and permit temptation to lure them into idolatry and disobedience.

In opposition to God, the serpent presents himself as a false lord offering a false word. He casts doubt on God's word: "Did God actually say . . . ?" He blatantly contradicts God: "You will not surely die." And he offers Eve a new interpretation of reality where God is not a loving covenant king, but a power-hungry, fearful, oppressive tyrant. In order to be like God, the serpent suggests, you must *defy* him. Of course, the irony is that humanity is already like God—bearing his image—in all the ways that truly matter and are appropriate for creatures, and they bear this image rightly only as they imitate him in obedient worship. But with one act of rebellion, they can become like God in a horrid and treasonous way, displacing the Creator and enshrining themselves on his throne. They become like God by trying to replace God.

At the heart of this rebellion is *idolatry*. Rather than loving, trusting, and obeying the God who made them for himself, Adam and Eve fix their hearts, hopes, and lives on created things—good things that they've made into gods. Power, freedom, control, status, and self are the false gods that captivate their imaginations and their worship, promising that *they're* the source of the good life, of true joy, of salvation. But like every idol that we worship in place of God, they bring with them striving instead of satisfaction, slavery instead of salvation.

It's worth noting the reversal of God's created order that this first sin involves. According to God's original design, he was Lord over his people, man was to lead his wife, and humanity was to exercise dominion over the rest of creation. But in Genesis 3, the serpent deceives the woman, who calls her husband to join, and they together violate God's word. Sin always involves a breach of God's created order, and it always brings further distortion, disarray, and disintegration into our lives.

Adam and Eve's first response to their sin is shame. No longer is there innocence, vulnerability, or openness because now they recognize the reality of their guilt. What follows are a number of creative attempts to deal with this stain of sin. They try to mask their shame with fig leaves, striving in vain to produce a manmade covering that will conceal their guilt from God and one another. They hide from the Lord in fear, hoping that they might escape his holy gaze. They shift blame by pointing the finger at everyone but themselves. Adam blames Eve, even implying that God is at fault for creating her ("The *woman* whom *you* gave to be with me, *she* gave me fruit of the tree, and I ate"[1]), while Eve blames the serpent. And our attempts at self-justification often take the same forms: covering our sin through our own efforts, fleeing God or denying his existence and authority, externalizing sin so that we can avoid taking responsibility by blaming our genes, our parents, our environment, and even God.

The Lord speaks a word of judgment—the curses of the covenant—to the covenant-breakers. To Eve God says that childbearing will bring with it increased pain. The marriage covenant will be marred by conflict as wives chafe against the call for loving submission and as husbands turn their responsibility to demonstrate sacrificial authority into an excuse for domineering abuses of power. To Adam God says that the ground will no longer flourish under his cultivation. Rather, all creation will experience a measure of futility as work becomes toilsome and often unproductive. Interestingly, as humanity seeks to fulfill their mandate to multiply (through childbearing) and exercise dominion over the earth (through cultivation), the sting of sin will be acutely felt. Ultimately, the very ground humanity was commissioned to work will swallow him up in death. But the death

---

1. Gen 3:12, emphasis added.

## The Fall of Man

is not merely physical. Adam and Eve are themselves expelled from the garden, exiled from the presence of the Lord, and this alienation from God is nothing less than spiritual death.

And yet in the midst of judgment, the Lord speaks a word of promise. He declares that there will be enmity between the seed of the serpent and the seed of the woman. Those who walk in the character of the serpent and those who walk in covenant with God by faith will stand in opposition to one another, and much of Genesis is concerned with tracing these two lines. More than this, God pronounces that a deliverer will arise from Eve who will bruise the serpent's head even as the serpent bruises his heel. In other words, somewhere along the line, the Lord will send one to destroy the works of the devil, and even though he will experience suffering at Satan's hands, he will deal the serpent a death blow from which he can never recover. In Genesis 3:15 then, we have the first promise of the gospel, a promise that's fulfilled when Jesus is betrayed and nailed to the cross in order to satisfy God's wrath against sin and restore his people to life with God.

Upon hearing these words, Adam calls his wife "Eve, because she was the mother of all living,"[2] an act of faith that demonstrates trust in God's promise to send a conquering offspring from her line. And in grace the Lord sacrifices an animal to cover them in a way their fig leaves never could. When we consider that in ancient cultures clothing someone in a garment was often a sign of covenant commitment,[3] it becomes clear that God is committing himself to a covenant of grace through which he'll bring restoration and reconciliation to this sinful and broken race.

In order that Adam and Eve might not eat of the tree of life and be confirmed to live eternally under the curse of sin and death, God sends them out of the garden and blocks the way to the tree of life. For now, all of life takes place east of Eden—outside of the immediate presence of the Lord, condemned in spiritual death, in a creation groaning under the curse of sin, where the blessings of salvation are experienced by faith and not by sight—and the only way back to the tree of life is to trust in the one who hung upon the tree of death.

*Gracious Father, when we look at your word, we not only hear the story of the world. We hear the story of our own hearts as well. Like our first parents, we set ourselves up as gods and seek to dethrone you. We fall prey to idols and*

---

2. Gen 3:20.
3. For example, see Ezek 16:8.

## Part One: From Creation to Christ

*lies that lead to false worship, disobedience, and the disintegration of relationships. But you have kept the promise you made, sending your Son to defeat the serpent through his sufferings. Grant us the faith to hope in Jesus and to rest in his finished work as we wait for the restoration of all creation when sin, death, and Satan are banished forever.*

# 4

# The Flood of Judgment

*Genesis 6:5–22; 8:13—9:17*

FOLLOWING GOD'S PROMISE OF a deliverer through the seed of the woman, the persistent question looming over the narrative is *Who will be this promised conqueror? When will this person emerge from among God's people?* Genesis traces this line of promise through Seth (the son given to Adam and Eve after Cain's murder of Abel),[1] and one of the major concerns of the book—and really the entire Old Testament—is to track the family line of God's covenant people and follow God's faithfulness to his promise.

Of course, the events of Genesis 3 have left their mark on the world. The effects of Adam and Eve's sin are immediately evident. By the time Seth's line arrives at Noah, the earth is full of wickedness, and even among the line of promise there are very few indications of consistent faithfulness: "The LORD saw that the wickedness of man was great in the earth, and that every intention of the thoughts of his heart was only evil continually."[2] Where only a few chapters ago God looked at his world and saw that it was good, now he sees that the wickedness of sin has infiltrated every dimension of human life. The human heart is naturally opposed to God—completely devoted to idolatry and self-salvation—and this false worship is unceasing in its intensity and results in violence toward neighbor. Envy, deception, aggression, oppression, and self-protection inevitably flow from hearts searching for life in gods that can't possibly deliver it. We'd be well

---

1. See Gen 4.
2. Gen 6:5.

## Part One: From Creation to Christ

served to consider how our own idolatry contributes to a similar kind of violence in our relationships as well.

So God pronounces judgment. Grieved by the sin that destroys the creatures and the creation that he loves, God elects to blot out man and the rest of world. This is a difficult declaration for modern people to hear: an angry God announcing judgment on the entire earth. This picture simply doesn't fit with most popular conceptions of a loving God.

But anger isn't opposed to love. It's *part of* love. Anger is the loving response to anything that threatens what we cherish. Of course, anger can be abusive and corrupt when we love the wrong things in the wrong proportion, but in the plot line of the Bible, God's wrath is shown to be the perfectly just *and* perfectly loving response of a holy God against the idolatry that's infinitely guilty because it dismisses his glory and wreaks havoc upon his world. To put it plainly, if God is truly a righteous God of justice, and if God actually treasures his glory, his people, and his creation, then he *must* do something about the sin that rejects him and ravages his world. A God who doesn't get angry is a God who doesn't care about justice. A God who doesn't get angry is a God who doesn't love. The appropriate question, then, isn't *How can God judge sin?* When our imaginations are shaped by God's story, the appropriate, awe-inducing question becomes *How can God offer mercy to anyone at all?*

And mercy is precisely what he offers. We're told that Noah found favor in the eyes of the Lord. In a world full of creatures exercising sinful independence, Noah walks with God. He trusts the word of the Lord, obeys him as sovereign King, and receives God's gracious promise of rescue. Noah is undoubtedly a sinner, and he surely deserves the same condemnation that's been pronounced on the rest of creation. But Noah is a sinner who walks in covenant with God, and the Lord will deliver him through the flood of his judgment to safety by grace. God instructs him to build an ark, and this ark will be the means by which God brings him and his family through the flood unharmed.

As the passage develops, it becomes clear that God isn't merely wiping out his former creation. He's actually *renewing the world*. The flood will destroy a world that's been horrifically marred by sin, but Noah and his family will be the start of a new humanity in a new creation. The animals Noah preserves in the ark will again fill the world, and Noah is commanded to be fruitful and multiply, a repetition of the initial mandate given to Adam and Eve. In fact, if you look closely, the parallels between Noah and Adam are

## The Flood of Judgment

quite striking, and they confirm that Noah is the head of a new humanity after God's judgment.

When the flood subsides, the Lord makes a covenant, promising that he'll never again destroy the world by flood even though "the intention of man's heart is evil from his youth."[3] While the flood was a renewal of the world in one sense, water alone isn't powerful enough to wipe away the sin that resides in every human heart. Though rebellion will continue, the Lord won't pour out cosmic judgment again until the Last Day, and until then he'll uphold the natural order and maintain his creation. This is sometimes referred to as a covenant of common grace. It promises God's gracious preservation of creation for all people, regardless of whether they worship him or not.

God offers a sign to confirm this covenant. He sets his bow in the clouds as a reminder to himself and to humanity that he has promised never to destroy all creation by flood again. Like a warrior setting aside his weapon, God lays down his bow because he won't approach the world as a warrior, but as a sustainer and, ultimately, as a Redeemer. When the beauty of the bow is seen against the raging darkness of the clouds, God will remember his covenant, and humanity can be assured that God's posture toward his world is one of preserving grace.

The biblical account of the flood brings us face-to-face yet again with God's justice and grace. The in-breaking justice we see in the flood is a foreshadowing, a precursor, a signpost looking ahead to the final judgment that awaits a rebellious world. Though God sustains his creation in common grace during this age, he'll one day judge sin in perfect wisdom, righteousness, and justice. Yet here in Genesis, God makes clear that judgment is neither the only word nor the last word. In the middle of this flood of justice against wickedness and idolatry, the Lord acts in grace to secure the salvation of Noah and his family. God won't forsake his promise to rescue his creation from the curse of sin and death, and he brings Noah safely through his judgment to begin afresh in a renewed world.

God's grace toward Noah shows us the pattern of God's saving activity, the way God works to rescue his people. By grace he brings sinners through judgment into salvation, but only when Jesus goes to the cross does this pattern find its ultimate fulfillment. On the cross, the dark storm clouds of holy wrath swallow Jesus up, and he receives the flood of God's judgment against sin so that sinners can be delivered into the salvation of life with

3. Gen 8:21.

## Part One: From Creation to Christ

God. By faith, Noah entered the ark and was saved. By faith, Christians enter into the sacrificial death and resurrection life of Jesus. The rescuing grace of Genesis 6–9 points us toward the gospel and the Christ through whom God will truly save his people, begin a new humanity, and restore the whole creation.

*Great God and Father of our Lord Jesus Christ, we've seen in your word the judgment that all sin deserves. Our hearts are wicked, and our idolatry so often leads to violence against you and others. Help us to look to Jesus for our rescue. In him, we're delivered safely through judgment and into communion with you. Give us the strength to rejoice in your faithfulness, celebrate your grace, and walk in worship, knowing that in Christ you have accomplished our redemption. Enable us to see Jesus as the fulfiller of your saving purposes and as the answer to our sinful hearts, and fill us with anticipation of the day when Christ will return to restore the whole world.*

# 5

# God's Covenant with Abram

## *Genesis 12:1–3; 15*

AFTER ADAM AND EVE'S covenant breaking in Genesis 3, God would have been perfectly justified in wiping out creation entirely. But he didn't. He made a promise of deliverance, and in Genesis 12, he puts that promise into action. The Lord speaks to a man named Abram, calls him to leave his homeland for the land God will show him, and makes a covenant promise to him. God's sovereign grace is here on full display, for while nothing in Abram merits God's favor or attention, the Lord willingly enters into a covenant relationship with him. The terms of this covenant are repeated numerous times in Genesis, and four major blessings consistently emerge:

1. *God will make Abram a great nation.* God will bless Abram with a family whose multitudes are virtually innumerable. In Genesis 17, God actually changes Abram's name to Abraham, which means "father of a multitude," in order to reflect his promise.
2. *God will give Abram a land.* Though he's called to leave his family and home behind to follow the Lord in faith, God will grant Abram and his descendants a place to dwell, a home. The Old Testament references to the "promised land" are built on this aspect of God's covenant.
3. *God will be their God, and they will be his people.* Not only will Abram be the father of a great nation who dwells in the land the Lord provides, but they'll have a special relationship to God. They will be his covenant people. That is, they will belong to the Lord as recipients of his gracious promises, and they will be obligated to love and serve him as his holy nation. And the Lord will be their covenant God who

gives himself to an undeserving people and promises his presence as he makes his dwelling among them.

4. *Through Abram, all the families of the earth will be blessed.* God's blessings won't be restricted to the biological family of Abram. Rather, somehow, some way, the Lord will make Abram's line the instrument of blessing to the entire world.

When we take all of these promised blessings together, it's clear that God's covenant with Abram is nothing less than a promise to restore the kingdom of God that was ruined at the fall. God will make a family with whom he dwells in covenant relationship in the home he gives, a family who will extend his blessings to all the nations of the earth. This is the essence of what Eden was all about, and God vows that he'll make it a reality even in the midst of a sin-scarred creation. From here until the end of the Old Testament, the story of God's redemptive work in the world will focus on the nation of Israel, Abram's descendants.

Yet, as all of us do, Abram doubts whether God's promise will actually come to pass. The Lord said that Abram would be a great nation, but by Genesis 15, he's still childless and wonders if his line will have to go through some other member of his household. The Lord assures Abram that his offspring will indeed be as bountiful as the stars in the heavens, and Genesis 15:6 offers that great statement of justification by faith: "And he believed the LORD, and he counted it to him as righteousness." Abram believed God's promise, and the Lord counted him righteous, holy, spotless, and pure *by faith*.

Still, Abram requires further reassurance. When God says that he'll give Abram a land, Abram replies, "O Lord GOD, how am I to know that I shall possess it?"[1] What follows is an elaborate—and for modern people quite confusing—ceremony, complete with sliced animals, a bloody walkway, a smoking fire pot, and a flaming torch. How is this in any way an answer to Abram's uncertainty?

In the ancient world, it was common when two parties made a covenant for them to ratify or seal the covenant with a ritual. In one such ritual, the parties slaughtered animals, divided up the pieces, and walked together between the carcasses, symbolically declaring that if they break the covenant, "may what happened to these animals happen to me." It was

---

1. Gen 15:8.

## God's Covenant with Abram

a physical way of making an oath and calling judgment on oneself should one break the covenant.

That's what's happening in Genesis 15. Animals are sacrificed and separated so that the covenant can be ratified on penalty of death. But there's a surprising twist. Normally, both parties of the covenant would walk through the pieces together. But here, *only God does*. The smoking fire pot and flaming torch—like the pillars of cloud and fire—are manifestations of God's presence as he walks alone down the bloody path between the carcasses.

Why does God go alone? Because his covenant with Abram is a covenant of grace. He made a one-sided promise that he would bless Abram, and nothing will stand in the way of him keeping his word. Abram wasn't deserving of God's attention when the Lord called him, and neither Abram nor anyone in his line merits God's continuing faithfulness. This is no give-and-take relationship—no manipulative *quid pro quo*—where God is cajoled into blessing by human goodness. Rather, God will keep his covenant as a gift of grace, and God's walking alone down the pathway demonstrates that God takes full responsibility for keeping these promises. God is symbolically saying, "If I fail to keep my word to you, Abram, may I die."

Only when we understand the central significance of God's covenant with Abram will we understand why the New Testament refers so frequently to the Abrahamic covenant when explaining the meaning of Jesus' life, death, and resurrection. Jesus is shown to be the truly righteous member of Abram's line who secures all the blessings of the covenant through his sacrificial death on the cross. In Genesis 15, God walks through the pieces to show that he would rather die than break his word. In Jesus Christ, God walks the lonely path to the cross where he *will* die in order to keep his word.

Each part of God's covenant with Abram finds its fulfillment in Jesus. God promised a great family, and all who trust Christ are grafted into God's covenant family, brought into Abram's line. God promised a land, and those who belong to Jesus will inherit not just a sliver of soil in the Middle East, but the entire world when God restores all of creation. God promised that he would be their God and they would be his people, dwelling together in covenant joy, and the church enjoys this unbreakable covenant bond, sealed by the presence of the Holy Spirit with us because of Jesus' atoning work. God promised that Abram's family would bless the nations, and Jesus opens

## Part One: From Creation to Christ

the way to God through his sacrifice so that every kind of person can know and belong to the Lord by faith.

In the unfolding story of God, Genesis 12 and 15 further clarify how the Lord will keep his promise to deliver creation from the curse of sin, and Jesus is the one who brings those promises to completion.

*Covenant God, we thank you that you initiated a relationship with a fallen world. You made a covenant of grace with Abraham, and you fulfilled that covenant in Jesus. The work is done. You've accomplished it all. Help us to live in the freedom of knowing that we don't contribute or add anything to the gracious salvation you've worked. When our hearts are uncertain and doubting whether you could accept us, help us to look to the cross of Christ where Jesus walked the road of death alone to cover our sin and bring us into your family. And let the joy of that grace push us into the world to declare your good news for all people.*

# 6

# The Sacrifice of Isaac

## *Genesis 22:1–18*

CHALLENGES TO GOD'S COVENANT with Abraham seem to emerge from every direction and threaten the fulfillment of God's promises. Sarah is taken as a wife of Pharaoh after a famine drives them to Egypt and Abraham lies to protect himself. Abraham permits Lot to take the more fertile territory when it becomes clear that the land can't sustain them both. Sarah is barren, and Abraham agrees to hurry things along by sleeping with her servant Hagar. Abimelech, the king of Gerar, tries to take Sarah in a scenario disturbingly similar to what happened in Egypt. Famine, cowardice, conflict, unbelief, and barrenness present obstacles to God's covenant. And one question towers above them all: How can God make a great nation of Abraham if he and Sarah can't even conceive a single child?

Despite these challenges, God keeps his word and gives Abraham and Sarah a son named Isaac. Finally, a ray of hope! But when Isaac is still only a young man, God does the unthinkable: he commands Abraham to offer his son as a sacrifice. Now *God himself* appears to be the greatest threat to the covenant! And yet Genesis gives us a clue that there's more here than meets the eye when it introduces this account by telling us that "God tested Abraham."[1] God is making a nearly impossible demand, one that initially can't be understood, so that Abraham will demonstrate whether or not he truly trusts God to keep his word.

This moment of crisis brings to the surface who Abraham is really trusting for life and joy. Does Abraham ultimately prize the giver or the

---

1. Gen 22:1.

gift? The blesser or the blessing? The God of the covenant or the benefits of the covenant? It's so easy for us to shift our allegiance away from God and start hoping in his good gifts in a disproportionate way. Our love for what God might give to or do for us begins to overshadow our love for God himself. And that's really the essence of idolatry. The first commandment (which will be given later on) is a call to have no other gods that compete with the one true God for our worship and trust. In this painful and confusing situation, where Abraham runs the risk of losing his son, Abraham's love and worship are revealed. Pay attention, because how *you* handle hardship and suffering will expose your heart, too.

The command for Abraham to sacrifice Isaac strikes modern ears as horrifically sadistic, but remember, the story of Scripture has already established that the penalty of Adam's sin is death. Not only is God the sovereign Creator who has the right to do with his creation as he pleases, but his creatures have sinned against him and are therefore under the curse of death. At a number of places in the Pentateuch (the first five books of the Old Testament), God reveals that death is the judgment for sin by demanding the life of the firstborn, who in that culture functioned as a representative of the entire family. In the Passover, the firstborn sons of Egypt are taken in God's judgment against sin, and in Exodus 13:11–16, God says that all the firstborn in Israel belong to him and must be redeemed through the sacrifice of a substitute animal. This Israelite practice will stand as an ongoing reminder of God's gracious deliverance in the exodus, but it also shows that the lives of sinners are forfeit before God and require redemption. In Genesis 22, God makes much the same point in requiring Isaac's life.

Abraham responds to the word of the Lord with faith and obedience. He tells a perplexed Isaac that God will provide for himself the lamb to be sacrificed. And when he draws near to the place of sacrifice, he says to the men with him, "I and the boy will go over there and worship *and come again to you.*"[2] Hebrews 11:17–19 explains Abraham's response: "By faith Abraham, when he was tested, offered up Isaac, and he who had received the promises was in the act of offering up his only son, of whom it was said, 'Through Isaac shall your offspring be named.' He considered that God was able even to raise him from the dead, from which, figuratively speaking, he did receive him back." God promised offspring through Isaac, and God commanded that Isaac be sacrificed. But Abraham obeys in the hope that God will be faithful to his covenant word and keep his promise even

---

2. Gen 22:5, emphasis added.

if it means having to bring Isaac back from the dead. Such faith in God's covenant, even when we can't see what God's doing or understand what's happening to us, is a necessary and defining part of the Christian life.

The climax of the story occurs as Abraham binds Isaac, places him on the altar, and lifts the knife over his boy. Just when it seems Isaac will indeed perish, the Lord intervenes and says, "Do not lay your hand on the boy or do anything to him, for now I know that you fear God, seeing you have not withheld your son, your only son, from me."[3] Just then, Abraham spots a ram caught in a thicket and offers it in place of his son, rejoicing that the Lord has indeed provided. Though God had every right to demand the life of a sinful human, *God himself provided the sacrifice that he required.* The God who made a promise of deliverance, who clothed Adam and Eve, and who walked the bloody path alone continues to reveal the way he will work on behalf of his people.

This passage is rich with important themes, and we would do well to ponder them deeply. But perhaps most fascinating is how this episode foreshadows for us the way God will ultimately work to redeem sinners. Moriah—where God provided the sacrifice—would become the site of Solomon's temple,[4] the place where sacrifices would be offered to atone for sin. But even more, God's gracious provision of a substitute for Isaac points to God's gracious provision of a substitute in the gospel. All of us deserve to die for our sins, but God provides the lamb for the sacrifice—the lamb of God, Jesus Christ. Rather than having Abraham offer up his beloved son, God the Father will offer *his* beloved Son in glorious fulfillment of his covenant of grace.

Walking with God in faith is seldom easy. Repenting of the idols that compete for our affection is often painful. Apparent obstacles to God's promises arise. But with the knowledge that God sent Jesus to be the promise keeping sacrifice for our sin, we can trust the Lord and offer him our worship and live with thanksgiving that our God is the God who provides.

*Father, you are abundantly gracious. We thank you for all the ways you've revealed yourself as our provider, and we rejoice that in Jesus you provided for our redemption. We owe you our very lives, but Jesus gave us his. Help us to see your glorious and merciful character and to walk in faith and faithfulness as your covenant people, trusting Jesus as the God and Savior who offered himself so that we might have life with you.*

3. Gen 22:12.
4. See 2 Chron 3:1.

# 7

# Slavery and the Promise of Rescue
## *Exodus 6:1–13*

After God's intervention to preserve Isaac's life, the rest of the book of Genesis traces the generations of Abraham's family and the passing on of God's covenant promises. God reaffirms his covenant with Abraham's son Isaac and Isaac's son Jacob. Genesis keeps our eyes firmly trained on the chosen family who will bring blessing to the nations, the family from whom God's promised deliverer will arrive.

But by the end of Genesis, Jacob and his twelve sons (who give rise to the twelve tribes of Israel) are in Egypt, a foreign land. The book of Exodus begins by recounting how, within a few generations, the fruitful and multiplying Israelite population begins to threaten Pharaoh's rule over Egypt, so he oppresses the Israelites and makes them slaves.

These events immediately raise afresh the perennial question of whether God will keep his covenant. He promised that Abraham's family would be a multitude who dwelled in the land God provided and that they would bless the world. But now they're slaves in a land that doesn't even belong to them. They can't even help themselves, so how will they bless the nations? Israel's captivity in Egypt is the greatest threat to the fulfillment of God's promises that we've seen so far in the Bible's story.

It's in these tumultuous circumstances that God raises up Moses to be his spokesperson and rescuing representative. Speaking to Moses through a bush that burns but isn't consumed, God tells Moses that he is the covenant Lord—the God of Abraham, Isaac, and Jacob, the I am—and he commands Moses to confront Pharaoh and bring his covenant people out of bondage. Though not without doubt and reservation, Moses eventually obeys and

## Slavery and the Promise of Rescue

journeys to Egypt with his brother Aaron. However, when their first foray into Pharaoh's court only prompts the king to make the Israelites' labor even more difficult, Moses is left lamenting that the Lord ever sent him in the first place.

"But the Lord said to Moses, 'Now you shall see what I shall do to Pharaoh . . .'"[1] God repeats the word he gave to Moses before: he will bring his people out from slavery, and nothing will stand in his way.

Verse 6 reveals how the Lord will accomplish this liberation: "I will bring you out from under the burdens of the Egyptians, and I will deliver you from slavery to them, and I will redeem you with an outstretched arm and with great acts of judgment." God's *deliverance* of Israel will take place through *judgment* of Egypt. The pattern that began with Genesis 3:15 and emerged again in the account of Noah's flood continues. God works salvation for his people by judging sin. He mercifully preserves them through his judgment and brings them to freedom.

In the events that follow, the Lord's judgment will be evident on a number of levels. In the ten plagues that precede the exodus, God will judge Egypt as a nation. The leaders, citizens, and structures of Egyptian society will experience God's wrath. At the same time, the Lord makes it clear that his judgment on Egypt is simultaneously directed at the gods the Egyptians worship.[2] The Egyptians honored deities related to the Nile River, the sun, and the earth, but the Lord turns the Nile to blood, plunges the land into darkness, and brings forth gnats from the dust of the ground. In fact, each of the plagues is a direct challenge to one or more of the gods of Egypt, demonstrating the Lord's supremacy over all idolatrous competitors. Finally, God's judgment rests upon Pharaoh himself, the king of Egypt. To the Egyptian mind, Pharaoh was a god-like figure, exercising divine authority from the throne. The plagues that ravage Egypt expose Pharaoh's utter weakness in comparison to God and reveal that the Lord is the only divine King, the only God who can truly save.

And yet, when given the Lord's words through Moses, the people of Israel don't listen "because of their broken spirit and harsh slavery."[3] Perhaps they think God can't possibly win a showdown with Pharaoh. Perhaps the security of slavery in Egypt is more appealing than the uncertainty of walking into freedom and trusting the Lord. The covenant people are slow

---

1. Exod 6:1.
2. See Exod 12:12; Num 33:4.
3. Exod 6:9.

to take hold of God's promises and would rather remain in bondage than hope in the God who guarantees their deliverance. Such is the way of sin. Though sin breaks our spirit with the harsh demands of slavery, it often seems far more easy and attractive to remain bound by our idols than to daily let go of our false masters and live in the freedom of communion with God. But not even Israel's slowness of heart will stop the Lord from saving.

If we look closely at this passage, we'll notice one more incredibly significant point. Within the short span of verses 2–8, God repeats four times the phrase "I am the Lord." Why should Moses believe God's promise? "I am the Lord." Why should Israel trust that deliverance will arrive? "I am the Lord." Why should all God's people have confidence that his covenant promises will be fulfilled? "I am the Lord."

This simple statement of God's identity begins and ends his conversation with Moses, serving as the foundational truth from which everything else arises. The ultimate reason God will keep his promise—the ultimate reason for Moses to persevere in hope—is God's own character. He made the covenant. He's eternally faithful to his word. He is the Lord. The strongest nation on earth, the most powerful man alive, the whole idol-laden pantheon of Egypt—none of these will stand in the way of God's covenant faithfulness. He will keep his word, and he'll work deliverance for his people.

And it's this same faithfulness that's at work when the Father sends his Son Jesus into the world and to the cross to bring his people out of their deepest slavery—the slavery to sin and death. At the cross, God shows his glory and supremacy over every power of darkness that opposes his rule and threatens his church. At the cross, God keeps his promise to make a people for his own possession in the fullest way, purchasing sinners and delivering them into fellowship with himself through the blood of Christ. And he does it because he is the Lord, the trustworthy and faithful God who makes and keeps the covenant.

*Our God and Father, the rescue that you worked for your people out of Egypt is but a foretaste of the rescue we've enjoyed in Jesus. You are the Lord who always remains faithful to his word, so fill us with faith that rests in your promises and lives joyfully from the conviction that your word is true. When our hearts are filled with doubt, recall to our minds that you are the Lord of the covenant and that no obstacle can stop your outstretched arm from accomplishing all that you've purposed to do. When we desire to hold on to our spirit breaking idols, grant us repentance so that we can let go of our false gods and trust the Christ who gives us true liberty. Take us to the cross where Jesus received the ultimate judgment that we might experience the ultimate salvation—freedom from the curse of sin to love and worship in communion with you.*

# 8

# The Passover and Exodus
## *Exodus 12:1–14, 29–42*

THE FEW CHAPTERS BETWEEN Exodus 6 and Exodus 12 summarize the events surrounding the first nine plagues of judgment on Egypt. Though Pharaoh has on a number of occasions expressed willingness to let the Israelites depart if only the plagues will stop, time and time again his heart is hardened, and he refuses to let God's people go free. The tenth and final plague serves as the climax of God's judging and saving purposes and also offers a remarkable glimpse into the meaning of redemption.

"So Moses said, 'Thus says the LORD: About midnight I will go out in the midst of Egypt, and every firstborn in the land of Egypt shall die, from the firstborn of Pharaoh who sits on his throne, even to the firstborn of the slave girl who is behind the handmill, and all the firstborn of the cattle.'"[1] The Lord vows to strike down every firstborn child in Egypt, but what about his people? Will God allow the children of his covenant to be swept up in his wrath on the Egyptians? The answer to this question is a gracious *no*. The Lord reveals that he'll pass over every household of Israel who trusts him and heeds his merciful word.

Each household is commanded to go out on the tenth day of the month and kill an unblemished, spotless lamb. They're to take the blood of the lamb and wipe it across their doorframe, roast the lamb over a fire, and eat the meat with unleavened bread and bitter herbs. The Lord gives specific instructions concerning how the lamb must be cooked and eaten, and he tells the people to eat it quickly with belts fastened, sandals on, and

---

1. Exod 11:4–5.

staffs in hand. They're dressed and ready for action because this is the Lord's Passover, and they must be prepared to move when he comes to liberate them from their slavery.

God promises that, when he sees the blood over each Israelite door, he'll pass over and preserve them from destruction. As the ram caught in the thicket meant mercy for the firstborn Isaac, the sacrificial lamb of the Passover means mercy for every firstborn in Israel. In themselves, there's nothing that sets the Israelites apart from the Egyptians. They're just as guilty of sin, just as tarnished by the fall, as anyone. But in his covenant faithfulness, God accepts the sacrifice of a spotless substitute so that his people might be safe from his righteous judgment. The blood marks the Israelites as covered. The lamb receives the death they deserve so that they can receive the life with God they never deserved.

When this plague comes to pass, "there was a great cry in Egypt, for there was not a house where someone was not dead"[2]—not even the palace of Pharaoh. In spite of Pharaoh's posturing as a god-like king, he's ultimately powerless in the face of the one true God and King. The firstborn son of Egypt's "divine" ruler has been snuffed out by the judgment of the God of Israelite slaves. The Lord has definitively demonstrated his sovereign superiority over Egypt and its gods.

Having witnessed the power of the Lord, the Egyptians send out the people of Israel. God's covenant family is finally free. The deliverance that God promised has at last come to pass as the Israelites make their way out of Egypt, liberated by the saving arm of the Lord. Pharaoh's final words are quite significant: "Up, go out from among my people, both you and the people of Israel; and go, *serve the Lord*, as you have said."[3] Paradoxically, Israel's freedom from slavery in Egypt is a freedom to service of God. Though this stands at odds with contemporary Western notions of freedom as total autonomy and unrestricted self-determination, the Bible emphasizes repeatedly in both the Old and New Testaments that the highest freedom any human can enjoy is the freedom to know, love, worship, trust, and obey the God who made us for covenant with himself—who made us to find our deepest longings met in him. Freedom *from* God is death, but freedom *with* God is the fullest kind of life imaginable.

As Israel journeys from Egypt, they'll be led by the Spirit of God himself in pillars of cloud and fire, and God will miraculously bring them

---

2. Exod 12:30.
3. Exod 12:31, emphasis added.

## Part One: From Creation to Christ

through the Red Sea as the waters part for his people and crash down upon the pursuing Egyptians. From now on, the Hebrew calendar will mark the month of the Passover as the first month, and the people will celebrate this feast every year as a memorial to teach and remind them that their God released them from the land of bondage, judged their oppressors, and poured out mercy on them in faithfulness to his promise to Abraham.

While the events of the Passover and exodus are defining moments in Israel's history and important developments in the redemptive story line of the Bible, they also point past themselves to a fuller, more complete, more glorious redemption. Though every sinner has earned death and condemnation from a holy God, the Lord sent his Son Jesus to be the ultimate Passover lamb whose shed blood covers the sins of God's people. Everyone who hides in faith under the sacrificial work of Christ is passed over, spared from judgment, a recipient of unmerited mercy. Pharaoh sacrificed his firstborn son in his self-serving and oppressive desire to maintain power, but the true God willingly offered up his firstborn Son as a gift of grace to purchase forgiveness, adoption, and life for unworthy people.

By his sacrifice, Jesus worked a deeper liberation—not from the bondage of physical slavery—but from the bondage of spiritual slavery to sin, idolatry, and death. In him, the church has walked a greater exodus from the kingdom of darkness into the kingdom of God's Beloved Son, where we're finally free to worship as servants of the living God. And at the Lord's Table, we too regularly celebrate a feast that testifies to us of the finished work of redemption in Jesus while we stay ready, awake, and watchful for the anticipated day when Christ returns and our salvation is fully revealed.

*Our great God and Father, your wisdom, righteousness, and grace are on glorious display in your redemptive workings in history. Just as you brought Israel out of Egypt on an exodus to freedom, you've brought your church from death to life—from slavery to sin and self into the liberating worship of your name—through Christ's resurrection. Give us thankful hearts as we dwell on your Son's willing sacrifice, which covers ours sin and reconciles us to you. Help us to walk in the freedom we've been granted, joyfully serving the one who's purchased us for himself.*

# 9

# The Ten Commandments

*Exodus 20:1–21*

AFTER BRINGING THE PEOPLE of Israel out of their bondage in Egypt through the miraculous events of the exodus, God leads the people to Mount Sinai. There he calls Moses to meet him on the mountain and delivers his law, and the most concise expression of this law is found in the Ten Commandments.

The form of the Ten Commandments very closely mirrors the covenants of the ancient world. There's a historical preamble that establishes the relationship between the two parties: "I am the LORD your God, who brought you out of the land of Egypt, out of the house of slavery."[1] God's commands to Israel are grounded both in his holy character as the covenant Lord and in his previous work to redeem them from slavery. Who God is and what God has done are the foundations for Israel's obedience to his word.

There are also covenant stipulations, laws that govern how the two parties relate to one another. As the rescued people of God, Israel is to live in covenant with God in all the ways that he's specified, and the body of the Ten Commandments briefly summarizes what faithfulness to God looks like. Obedience to the covenant will bring blessings on Israel as a nation, and disobedience will bring curses upon the people.

In order to understand how the story of Scripture develops from here, we've got to see how this covenant arrangement relates to the covenant God already made with Abraham. The Abrahamic covenant was a covenant of

---

1. Exod 20:2.

grace where God promised to single-handedly restore his kingdom and bring salvation to the nations. But the covenant at Sinai (often referred to as the Mosaic covenant) is a covenant of works, a covenant where Israel must obey in order to experience national blessing. The Abrahamic covenant guaranteed that God will restore his kingdom, and the Mosaic covenant reveals that these blessings will only be granted to Israel if they walk in covenant with God in holiness, obedience, and worship. One of the most dramatic tensions in the Old Testament involves how God can keep his promise to Abraham when Israel keeps on violating his law and bringing about the curses of the covenant. Only when Jesus enters the picture as the descendant of Abraham who perfectly fulfills God's law will this tension finally be resolved.

Space doesn't permit a detailed exposition of the significance of each command, but a few guiding principles will help us read the Ten Commandments rightly:

1. *Love of God and love of neighbor*—The commandments have traditionally been divided into two tables. The first table (commands one through four) deals with our obligations toward God, and the second table (commands five through ten) concerns how the people of God treat other human beings. Jesus' summary of the law similarly emphasizes the love of God and love of neighbor: "You shall love the Lord your God with all your heart and with all your soul and with all your mind. This is the great and first commandment. And a second is like it: You shall love your neighbor as yourself. On these two commandments depend all the Law and the Prophets."[2] Together, the two tables summarize the life of worship and love that is appropriate for creatures who live in covenant with their holy Creator.

2. *Negative prohibitions and positive requirements*—While most of the commands are given as prohibitions ("You shall not"), each prohibition carries with it a corresponding positive requirement. The first commandment doesn't just outlaw the idolatrous worship of other gods. It requires that faithful love, trust, and obedience be given completely and solely to the covenant Lord. The ninth commandment doesn't merely forbid false witness against your neighbor. It demands that all speech be loving and truthful, just as God's speech is.

---

2. Matt 22:37–40.

3. *An entire vision of life*—Each command actually serves as a lens through which we can interpret all of life. At the most specific level, the third command deals with the way one speaks the name of God. However, if the covenant people of God bear God's name throughout life, then all of existence is an opportunity to glorify the name of God, and all sin is therefore a taking of God's name in vain. Similarly, the eighth commandment specifically prohibits stealing a neighbor's goods. But whenever we sin, we're stealing glory and worship from God, and we're often stealing from our neighbors the respect, dignity, and love that they deserve as God's image bearers. So all of life can be viewed through the unique perspective of each command. We would be well served to walk slowly and carefully through each of the commands, contemplating what each requires, how all of life falls under the umbrella of every commandment, and how the piercing mirror of God's law exposes sin and idolatry we never even knew we had.

With this perspective, we see how deep God's law actually goes—all the way to the heart. The Ten Commandments call for a whole life of worship in faithfulness to God, down to our most basic motives and fundamental loves. This law reveals our sin. It shows us all the ways we fail to rightly obey the Lord, helping prompt regular patterns of honest, self-critical confession and repentance. *But it does more.* God's law also points us to Jesus, the only perfectly faithful human who kept all of God's commands.

Israel couldn't keep the entire law, and neither can we. But where we've fallen short of the whole life of comprehensive holiness and devotion that God requires, Jesus has gloriously prevailed. Jesus embodied perfect holiness, and he gives his holiness to everyone who trusts him. And this means that coming face-to-face with the Ten Commandments will simultaneously make you more realistically humble and more invincibly secure than you've ever been.

But in this beautiful dance called the Christian life, when God's law drives you to God's gospel, his gospel leads you back to his law with a new vitality—a new power for worshipful obedience. Only when we rest in the gospel promise that Jesus' righteousness has been counted toward us will we have the thanksgiving, security, and joy to say no to our weak idols and gladly say yes to God for the glory of his name. As we trust Christ for our righteousness and life, we can look to God's law in the Ten Commandments to direct us in the truly good life—the flourishing life of worship that God desires for his rescued children.

## Part One: From Creation to Christ

*Father, your law shows us the holiness that's necessary to enter into your presence. If we were left to ourselves, we would remain under the curse of sin, always and only deserving to be exiled from you. Give us ears to hear the deep demands of your law. Give us hearts that are ready to confess our sin in repentance. Give us eyes that look to Jesus as the fully obedient servant. And, rejoicing in the holiness and grace of Christ, enable us to live in your world according to your word.*

# 10

# Blessings, Curses, and Forgiveness
## *Deuteronomy 28:1–6, 15–19; 30:1–6*

THE EVENTS SURROUNDING ISRAEL'S exodus from Egypt and the giving of the Ten Commandments at Sinai seem to suggest that the covenant people have a bright future ahead. Having witnessed the powerful and gracious faithfulness of God, and having received the very words of their King, surely Israel will go forth honoring the Lord in trust and grateful submission. But it is not so. The infiltrating disease of sin pervades the deepest recesses of the human heart, and no sooner does Moses come down from the mountain than the people have constructed a golden calf to worship. Unfortunately, this sort of idolatrous wavering will be part of Israel's normal experience, and they spend forty years stranded in the wilderness before God permits them to enter the Promised Land.

Now, Israel stands on the cusp of the land that God promised to give to Abraham, and the book of Deuteronomy records Moses' words to the people as they prepare to enter. Deuteronomy revisits the covenant stipulations from Sinai and calls Israel to renew their covenant with the Lord as they set foot into this new stage in their national history. Like the Ten Commandments, the whole book of Deuteronomy resembles the structure of ancient covenants, emphasizing yet again that Israel possesses a special relationship with God and that they must honor him in every way as their sovereign Lord.

After spending many chapters outlining general and specific laws, Deuteronomy 28 expresses the consequences for both obedience and disobedience. If the people "faithfully obey the voice of the LORD,"[1] they'll enjoy national blessing: social peace, political justice, agricultural abundance, reproductive fruitfulness, military victory, economic prosperity. All these physical blessings draw our imaginations back to Eden, because as Israel walks in covenant with God, they'll experience and witness to the *shalom* of life with God. These blessings are a foretaste of the restoration of God's kingdom.

But if Israel rebels against the Lord and turns her back on his commands, then curses will overtake them as the just punishment for their covenant breaking idolatry. The extended description of the curses in Deuteronomy 28:15–68 is quite graphic, and in some places difficult to even read. Yet in the midst of all the horrific dimensions of these curses, perhaps the most daunting for a nation hoping to participate in the establishment of God's healing rule in the world would be the threat of exile. Exile under a foreign power would be understood as nothing less than a return to the bondage of Egypt, an enormous step away from the realization of God's promises.

Deuteronomy 30 begins, "And *when* all these things come upon you, the blessing and the curse, which I have set before you, and you call them to mind *among all the nations* where the LORD your God has driven you . . ."[2] Moses assumes—or prophetically foretells—that Israel will receive the previously mentioned curses for breaking the covenant. They'll be exiled under foreign powers, not because of the random turns of political history, but because the Lord will sovereignly drive them among the nations just as he threatened in the covenant. Yet, when all these things have come upon them, if Israel returns to the Lord in repentance and keeps the terms of their covenant with God, he'll show mercy, gather his people again from among the peoples where they've been scattered, and restore them.

This passage establishes the pattern of Israel's experience and helps us understand the developments that take place in the remainder of the Old Testament. Broadly speaking, Israel's history can be interpreted as repeating cycles of blessing and prosperity, judgment for idolatry and disobedience, and restoration upon repenting and turning to the Lord. Deuteronomy offers us a covenantal perspective of the rest of the Old Testament narrative.

At this point in Scripture, an ominous cloud hangs over the story. If the uninterrupted blessings of fellowship with God, if the restoration of

1. Deut 28:1.
2. Deut 30:1, emphasis added.

what was lost in Eden, if the kingdom the Lord promised to Abraham, can only be secured by perfect, whole-life obedience to God's law, then it only stands to reason that such blessing will never fully come about. Sin-stained people simply aren't capable of this sort of faithfulness. But Deuteronomy 30:6 hints at a solution. One day, the Lord will circumcise the hearts of his people so that they can love him and follow him and live. God will give his covenant people new hearts, and the blessings—not the curses—of the covenant will be theirs. Only as the story continues will God reveal just how this can be.

It would be a grave error for Christians on this side of the cross to read these texts as if they were spoken directly to us. This covenant arrangement was given to Israel, not to individual Christians or to political nations today, so we can't simply insert ourselves into these passages. We must read these texts through the lens of Jesus' death and resurrection. We must apply these texts to ourselves through the mediating work of Christ.

In his life of glad worship and obedience to God, Jesus merited all of the blessings of the covenant. In his suffering for the sins of his people, Jesus received all the curses that the covenant demanded. Jesus underwent the deepest exile imaginable so that God could shower the covenant blessings on his children in grace. When the Holy Spirit unites sinners to Christ by faith, he unites us to Jesus' resurrection life, and God grants us new, circumcised hearts that are finally able to love him and walk in his ways, motivated by the freedom, joy, and thanksgiving of being accepted by grace. The church is the family where God's heart-restoring work has broken into a broken world, and because of Christ, the *shalom* of life with God is the reality in which this family lives by faith.

*Merciful, just, and holy God, when we hear of your covenant with Israel, we acknowledge that we've earned none of the blessings and all of the curses. But when we hear the precious message of the gospel, we rejoice that Jesus accepted all of the curses so that we could live in your blessing. Draw our trust and worship to Jesus—the truly faithful Israelite, the perfectly obedient covenant servant—so that we might rest in the security of your acceptance and, with circumcised hearts, live from this new identity in love for you.*

# 11

# The Covenant with David

## 2 Samuel 7:1–17

Much takes place between the end of Deuteronomy and the early chapters of 2 Samuel. Moses dies. Joshua leads the people to drive out the inhabitants of Canaan under the Lord's direction. A series of judges exercises leadership over Israel. Cycles of idolatry, judgment, repentance, and deliverance form a disturbingly predictable pattern. Finally, the people clamor for a king so that they can be "like all the nations,"[1] and this desire to be *like* the nations is a far cry from their call to live as a *light* to the nations that's distinguished by their faith in and devotion to God. The Lord makes Saul the first king over Israel, but Saul fails to rule righteously or lead the people into faithfulness. As a result, the Lord anoints a shepherd boy named David to succeed Saul as king.

The highs and lows of David's reign deserve study in their own right, but our passage in 2 Samuel 7 narrates the central event of David's entire kingship, the moment that establishes David as the most significant king in Israel's history. Since giving Moses his law on Mount Sinai, the Lord had made his dwelling among his people in a tent (often referred to as the "tabernacle") that could be moved from place to place as the people journeyed. When David compares his palatial home of cedar with God's tent, his intentions are clear. He wants to build a more permanent house for God.

This seems a noble desire, but the word of the Lord comes to the prophet Nathan and offers a surprising response: God won't allow David to build his temple. A few themes emerge in God's reply:

---

1. 1 Sam 8:5.

## The Covenant with David

1. *The Lord doesn't need human help.* Verse 5 almost carries the tone, "Would *you* build me a house to dwell in?" God has been perfectly content to live in the tent that he commanded the Israelites to build, and he doesn't require the assistance—however well-intentioned—of his people. Behind David's plan, there seems to be an inadequate understanding of God's self-sufficient completeness and humanity's weakness.

2. *God determines how his people worship him.* Verse 7 makes it clear that the Lord never asked any of Israel's leaders to construct a temple for him, and the implication is that it's inappropriate for anyone, even the king, to independently determine how he will worship God. The second commandment teaches that God's covenant people should only worship him in the ways he has prescribed. So the Lord won't permit David to simply decide to build him a dwelling place apart from his divine command.

3. *Most importantly, God's response demonstrates that he is the God who serves and blesses his people in grace.* There is a beautiful play on words here: David wants to build a house (a physical structure) for the Lord, but the Lord vows to build a house (a royal dynasty) for David! God will grant David a great name and give Israel peace. After David, the Lord will raise up his offspring and establish his kingdom. David's offspring will build God's temple, and this former shepherd's house and kingdom will stand forever. The God whom David is obligated to serve elects to serve him. The God whom David feels he ought to bless with a house elects to bless David with a house that will never perish from the earth.

In the sweep of redemptive history, God's covenant promise to David is enormously significant. This covenant further clarifies how God will keep the promises he originally made to provide a deliverer and restore his kingdom on the earth. He'll do it through a king from the line of David. Additionally, God's words here inaugurate the Davidic dynasty and establish a hope for the future that the Old Testament returns to again and again: God will bring an eternal kingdom, ruled over by a son from David's royal family. In light of this promise, David is held up as a type—a model—of the coming Messiah, a precursor who shows what this future king will be like. And in the immediate context, this covenant sets the stage for the building of the temple in Jerusalem.

## Part One: From Creation to Christ

But who fulfills this promise? At one level, Solomon does. Solomon is David's son. He constructs a temple for the Lord. He's disciplined for his iniquity, but God doesn't withdraw his steadfast love. But at another level, these promises are too grand and expansive to merely have Solomon in view. Even in the Old Testament, after Solomon's reign has long ended, the Lord refers to his covenant with David as the basis for his faithfulness and redeeming works.[2] And in the Gospels, the people of Israel are still searching for their Davidic prince who will sit on the throne forever.

When you read the Bible with an understanding of God's covenant with David, the first sentence of the New Testament absolutely explodes with new meaning: "The book of the genealogy of Jesus Christ, *the son of David*, the son of Abraham."[3] With the very first words of his Gospel, Matthew makes it clear that Jesus is the son of David who will inherit the throne and set up a never-ending kingdom and the son of Abraham who will extend blessing to the nations. Jesus will be the temple—the very presence of God among his people—and will build the church, a temple of living stones who are indwelt by his Holy Spirit. By his death and resurrection for sin, Jesus will introduce his kingdom into the world, a kingdom of restoration and peace with God. And because he's an eternal King, he's the only one qualified to truly reign over an eternal kingdom. In Christ, the Lord's covenant with David has its fullest and most glorious fulfillment.

*Gracious Lord, we often think of you as a God in need of our assistance, a God who will be made more complete by our service. Yet the chief way that you've called us to serve you is by laying down our efforts and allowing you to serve us in grace. Your promise to David is more than just a promise to bless him. It's a promise to bless the world through the sure establishment of your kingdom. Help us to repent of our personal kingdom-building, to rest in the work of King Jesus, to live from our citizenship in his kingdom, and to hope for the day when his glorious reign over all creation extends from sea to sea and out through eternity.*

---

2. Ezek 34:23–24 is one such example.
3. Matt 1:1, emphasis added.

# 12

# The Temple of God

## 2 Chronicles 6:12–21; 7:1–3, 11–22

THE LORD PROMISED THAT David's son would build a house in which God would dwell. At the beginning of 2 Chronicles, that promise comes to fruition as Solomon erects a temple for the Lord. When construction is completed, the king prays to the Lord and dedicates the temple to God's purposes. Solomon's prayer and the response from the Lord that follows together reveal a number of important themes.

Solomon notes that God has been faithful to keep part of the covenant he swore to David by permitting him to establish the temple. But he also makes a request: "Now therefore, O LORD, God of Israel, keep for your servant David my father what you have promised him, saying, 'You shall not lack a man to sit before me on the throne of Israel, if only your sons pay close attention to their way, to walk in my law as you have walked before me.'"[1] In 2 Samuel 7, God made an unconditional promise that one of David's descendants would inherit the throne forever. There, the Lord said that he would discipline iniquity, but he wouldn't withdraw his love. Here, Solomon petitions God to make good on the promise to preserve the royal line while recognizing that disobedience to God's law will mean the removal of David's offspring from the throne.

*How can both of these things be?* How can God say that he'll punish disobedience, and at the very same time promise that David's line will sit on the throne forever? Solomon eventually embraces unrighteousness, and as Israel's history progresses, the number of unjust and idolatrous kings far

---

1. 2 Chron 6:16.

outweighs those who walk with God, leading to the uprooting of David's dynasty as God's people are sent into exile. If there are no kings who will walk in the law, how will the covenant be kept? The answer is ultimately found in Jesus, the true Davidic King. He alone perfectly honors the law. He alone upholds the commands that God laid out for the king. He alone leads God's people as the covenant Son of God. God's promise to David is unconditional because Jesus keeps all the conditions. And this Jesus will reign forever.

Even in Solomon's dedicatory prayer, there's still an element of amazed disbelief that God would reside among his people: "But will God indeed dwell with man on the earth? Behold, heaven and the highest heaven cannot contain you, how much less this house that I have built!"[2] If not even heaven can contain the glory of the Lord, how will he live in a finite space constructed by men? Of course, God isn't contained by the temple, but he lowers himself in grace to live with his covenant people. The Lord walked with Adam and Eve in Eden. He led the captives on their journey from Egypt as a pillar of cloud and fire. He made the tabernacle his temporary dwelling place. And now God's name rests on the temple in Jerusalem, and the glory of the Lord fills the place.

All of this shows us that God desires to be with his people. His intention in creation was to dwell with the creatures who bore his image and worshipped him in holiness, and not even sin could stand in the way of God making that a reality. The apostle John would one day write of Jesus, "And the Word became flesh and dwelt among us, and we have seen his glory, glory as of the only Son from the Father, full of grace and truth."[3] In Jesus, God entered creation in flesh and blood and made his home among men, and the glory of God was truly present for humanity to see. The temple in Jerusalem demonstrates that God is set on having fellowship with his people. And through Christ, the final temple, God lived with his people for a time to accomplish the work that would secure our fellowship with him for eternity.

In the Old Testament, the temple was the center of Israelite religion. Not only was the temple the focus of Israel's prayer life—the place in which or toward which they were called to pray. It was also a house of sacrifice, where the priests in Israel were to make offerings to the Lord on behalf of

---

2. 2 Chron 6:18.
3. John 1:14.

## The Temple of God

the people. To put it plainly, the temple was the place where God's people met with their Lord. Through the temple, the people communed with God.

In the New Testament, a radical shift occurs. No longer do God's people worship God, pray to him, or find reconciliation with him through a brick and mortar temple. Jesus is the true temple, and he's therefore the center of every Christian's relationship with God. He's the sacrifice for sin that purchases our reconciliation. He's the mediator in whose name we pray. He's the priest who grants us access to the Father and welcomes us into the joy of fellowship with the triune God. Everything that the temple meant for Israel, Jesus means for the church. And the church, reconciled to God in Jesus Christ, is made into a temple as well, for the Lord blesses us with the presence of his indwelling Holy Spirit as a guarantee of the full salvation and communion with God we'll one day enjoy when Jesus returns to transform the entire creation into a holy temple for the glory of the Lord.

*Our God and Father, we don't meet with you in a physical house, but in the person of your Son, who took on flesh so that he might dwell with us and show us your glory. Exalt Jesus in our hearts as the Son who brings us to the Father, reconciles us through his sacrifice, and ensures that one day we'll make our eternal home in your presence. Fix our worship on the King whose rule will never end. Help us to commune with you through Christ by faith, enjoying the sweetness of your grace and fellowship, this day and always.*

# 13

# A Baby and a Branch

*Isaiah 9:2-7; 11:1-10*

THE REIGNS OF DAVID and Solomon were certainly the high points of Israel's national existence. Under those kings, Israel provided a pattern for the kingdom of God and established an expectation for what life would be like when God finished his redeeming work and ruled over his people. A just king sat on the throne; the people were free from their oppressors; God dwelt in the midst of his people—these are the contours of the blessed kingdom that God's people long for and that Jesus establishes.

Toward the end of Solomon's kingship, Israel began its descent into increasing unrighteousness, injustice, and idolatry. The nation splintered into a northern and southern kingdom, and God sent prophets to remind them of the Mosaic covenant, call them to repentance, and warn them of the dangers that awaited should they continue in their sin. In this context, Isaiah is commissioned by God to speak, and while much of his ministry deals with the threats and reality of exile, two passages in particular look toward the deliverance and restoration that God vows to bring.

The prophetic promises of Isaiah 9:2-7 and 11:1-10 use two different images—a baby and a branch—to communicate a number of overlapping themes. While each passage certainly has its own unique emphases, there are four common threads that are worthy of our attention.

# A Baby and a Branch

## Unexpected Hope

Into spiritual darkness, a light will burst forth and shine on God's people. Into a creation characterized by rejection of God and lives of sinful independence and rebellion, God's grace will break in with joy and salvation for undeserving people. Though it seemed darkness would remain forever, light will erupt into the blackness and bring with it the true knowledge of God. It's no wonder that the apostle John writes of Jesus, recalling Isaiah's words, "The light shines in the darkness, and the darkness has not overcome it."[1]

But the unexpected nature of God's saving work is also evident in Isaiah's description of the "stump of Jesse."[2] Jesse was David's father, and in light of God's covenant, one would expect a blossoming family tree. God's judgment on Israel, however, will leave this family tree as nothing but a stump. Yet from this stump—fruitless though it may appear—a shoot will spring forth, a descendant from the family line that will fulfill all of God's promises. In the darkest, most hopeless of circumstances, God will be faithful to keep his word.

## The End of Oppression

The burden and oppression experienced by Israel in exile will be broken as God ushers his people into true liberty. The branch, upon whom the Spirit of God rests, will fear the Lord, exercise righteousness for the poor, act equitably toward the meek, and strike down wickedness in justice. In his Sermon on the Mount, Jesus blessed the poor and the meek who trust in God, and he announced before the synagogue, "The Spirit of the Lord is upon me, because he has anointed me to proclaim good news to the poor. He has sent me to proclaim liberty to the captives and recovering of sight to the blind, to set at liberty those who are oppressed, to proclaim the year of the Lord's favor."[3] In these ways, Jesus was declaring that he is the promised one who has come to put an end to all oppression and bring his followers into the freedom of restored life with God.

---

1. John 1:5.
2. Isa 11:1.
3. Luke 4:18–19, where Jesus is quoting Isa 61:1–2.

PART ONE: FROM CREATION TO CHRIST

## Total, Cosmic Peace

Warriors' boots and bloody garments will be burned and destroyed. Isaiah 11 uses imagery from the animal world to make much the same point. It was not uncommon to use predatory beasts as illustrations of powerful and violent nations, so when Isaiah looks forward to the day when "the wolf shall dwell with the lamb, and the leopard shall lie down with the young goat,"[4] he's likely using figurative language to paint a picture of complete, global peace—the absence of war and the presence of *shalom*. "And a little child shall lead them,"[5] for in Christ, who stepped into his creation in the humblest possible way, the divisions and hostilities that plague humanity are finally healed. In Christ, people from every tribe and nation and tongue are reconciled to one another and to God. And the terrors and destructions of sin will have no place in Jesus' finished kingdom.

## The Long-Awaited King

God will bring these promises of cosmic restoration and salvation to fulfillment through the Davidic Messiah. A child will be given to God's people. The one to bear the titles of Wonderful Counselor, Mighty God, Everlasting Father, and Prince of Peace will be none other than the King who sits on the throne of David from this time forth and forevermore, of whose rule and reign there will be no end. The nations will inquire about this "root of Jesse"[6]—this child from David's royal line—and by faith in Christ they'll actually be grafted into God's kingdom family and welcomed to enjoy the glorious rest of knowing and belonging to God.

Isaiah 9 and 11 beautifully proclaim that God's salvation is coming for those who wait on the Lord. In Jesus, we've seen the fulfillment of these promises, and so as members of his kingdom now we live in the reality of Christ's accomplishments and wait for the day when he returns to consummate his kingdom and renew the whole world, when "the earth will be full of the knowledge of the Lord as the waters cover the sea."[7]

---

4. Isa 11:6.
5. Isa 11:6.
6. Isa 11:10.
7. Isa 11:9.

## A Baby and a Branch

*Holy God, we stand in awe of the beauty of your promises to unworthy creatures like us. We long for restoration. We yearn for a world where justice takes the place of oppression, where we're completely free from sin rather than shackled to our idols, where peace reigns and violence has ceased. We hunger for a new creation, where the true knowledge of your glory and grace fills all things. The promises you made through Isaiah, you've kept in Jesus. So help us to live in thanksgiving, worship, and hope as we celebrate the gospel of our Lord and anticipate his return to renew all of creation, including us.*

# 14

# The Suffering Servant of the Lord

*Isaiah 52:13—53:12*

THE FIRST THIRTY-NINE CHAPTERS of Isaiah deal primarily with events that took place during Isaiah's ministry (from the late 700s to the early 600s BC). Our text, however, comes from a section of Isaiah's prophecy that looks ahead and addresses future Israelites who would experience exile at the hands of the Babylonian empire during the 500s BC. God had warned his people that their disobedience to the Mosaic covenant would bring curses, and the nation's captivity to Babylon is a dramatic expression of God's judgment on the covenant breaking people. Yet, to those in exile who would likely wonder if God had abandoned his promises completely, the Lord makes a staggering declaration of grace that serves as one of the most remarkable expositions of the gospel in the entire Old Testament.

This passage focuses on a figure whom the Lord calls "my servant."[1] A look back at the story of the Bible up to this point will help us grasp the meaning of this term. Adam was created in the image of God to live as a covenant servant of the Lord—to obey God's word and reflect his character as he lived in covenant relationship with the Lord. Israel as a nation was also called to live faithfully as a covenant servant who walked with God and kept his word. Of course, neither Adam nor Israel was able to fulfill this calling, leaving us with the burning question, *Who can keep covenant with God? How can God bless those who deserve curses because of their sin?* Isaiah here provides us with the beginnings of an answer: God's servant will

---

1. Isa 52:13.

represent God's people as he walks in covenant with the Lord and willingly accepts their guilt.

Throughout this passage, the servant is described in language that recalls Israel's sacrificial system. The servant goes "like a lamb that is led to the slaughter"[2] to take the iniquity of the people, bring healing with his wounds, and sprinkle many nations to make them clean. To understand the true significance of these descriptions, we have to go back to the ram that the Lord provided in the thicket to be sacrificed in place of Isaac. We have to return to the Passover lamb whose blood marked the doors of the Israelite houses to protect them from judgment. We have to revisit the old covenant ceremonies where priests would offer the blood of animals so that the people might have their guilt cleansed in God's sight.

Isaiah shows us that those sacrificial substitutes were only a foretaste of God's guilt-pardoning redemption. The ultimate sacrifice—the true servant of the Lord—is no animal standing in place of men, but a human being who gives his life in place of his brothers and sisters. He bears our griefs and sorrows. He's pierced for our transgressions. He's crushed for our iniquities. Though he was spotless, having done no violence and without an ounce of deceit in his mouth, the faithful servant bears the punishment that sin deserves in order to make an offering for guilt. The sinless servant receives the chastisement due to covenant breakers so that God's peace might be upon them, rather than his judgment—so that God's healing grace might be poured out, rather than his wrath. Many are accounted righteous because the servant gives them his righteousness as he takes on their sin. And while an animal would have to be tied up and subdued to serve as a sacrifice, God's servant willingly enters into death, refusing to even open his mouth in objection, so that his people might have life.

This glorious promise also challenges us with the mysterious workings of God's providence. The servant is beaten, despised, rejected, and slain by men. Human beings oppress and destroy the servant, but they aren't really the primary actors in this prophetic drama—God is. "It was the will of the Lord to crush him; he has put him to grief."[3] "We esteemed him stricken, smitten by God, and afflicted."[4] "The Lord has laid on him the iniquity of us all."[5]

2. Isa 53:7.
3. Isa 53:10.
4. Isa 53:4.
5. Isa 53:6.

In, through, and underneath the murderous wickedness of men, the sovereign God of all history is working out his purposes for salvation. Human hands kill the Lord's servant, but all that happens is by the will of God and serves his redemptive goals. In his wisdom, the Lord uses the sin of rebels to bring forgiveness for rebels' sins.

And yet the servant's death isn't the servant's end. Isaiah tells us from the beginning that "he shall be high and lifted up, and shall be exalted."[6] But if the servant is crushed, then how can that happen? "When his soul makes an offering for guilt, he shall see his offspring; he shall prolong his days."[7] Though he offers himself as a willing sacrifice, pouring out his soul to death, he will yet live. Indeed, it's precisely *because* the servant is obedient all the way to death that the Lord gives him the inheritance of eternal life: "Therefore I will divide him a portion with the many, and he shall divide the spoil with the strong, because he poured out his soul to death and was numbered with the transgressors."[8]

The perfect covenant servant volunteers to receive the curse of death, but he can't be conquered by death because he has never disobeyed—the curse has no hold on him. God promised in Genesis that Eve's offspring would triumph though the serpent would strike him. Here, the Lord confirms that, though his servant is led to death, he'll be exalted in victorious life.

You can't read the New Testament without hearing echoes of this passage. That's because Jesus is so clearly God's fulfillment of Isaiah's promise. Jesus identified himself as the suffering servant of the Lord when he told his disciples that "even the Son of Man came not to be served but to serve, and to give his life as a ransom for many."[9] The Lord crushed Jesus at the cross so that he wouldn't have to crush us. Precisely because Jesus suffered for us as God's servant, the apostle Peter calls believers to suffer injustice with faith and grace:

> For to this you have been called, because Christ also suffered for you, leaving you an example, so that you might follow in his steps. He committed no sin, neither was deceit found in his mouth. When he was reviled, he did not revile in return; when he suffered, he did not threaten, but continued entrusting himself to him who

6. Isa 52:13.
7. Isa 53:10.
8. Isa 53:12.
9. Mark 10:45.

## The Suffering Servant of the Lord

judges justly. He himself bore our sins in his body on the tree, that we might die to sin and live to righteousness. By his wounds you have been healed. For you were straying like sheep, but have now returned to the Shepherd and Overseer of your souls.[10]

And this Christ who offered himself as a sacrifice for sin has been exalted by God in his resurrection and ascension to the throne so that all who trust in him might inherit a never-ending life of fellowship with God.

*Father, we thank you that where we could never keep covenant with you, you sent your only Son into the world to be the faithful servant in our place. We praise you for the grace you promised through Isaiah and have made a reality in the life, death, and resurrection of Jesus. Help us see how undeserving we truly are of such kindness so that our hearts may rejoice in the good news of the gospel and be filled with thankful love for our Savior and King. When we doubt our standing before you, and when we long to go our own way, strengthen us with the message that Jesus is our righteousness, the Good Shepherd who died for straying sheep that we might be returned to fellowship with you.*

---

10. I Pet 2:21–25.

# 15

# The New Covenant
*Jeremiah 31:31–34; Ezekiel 36:16–36*

As the Old Testament draws to a close, confidence in God's promises of restoration seems to have been replaced with jaded resignation. The glory days of David have passed. The nation has been driven into exile. The people have received the curses of the Mosaic covenant for their idolatry and disobedience. The kingdom of God as promised to Abraham seems an unattainable dream, for the covenant at Sinai made it clear that God will only dwell with the righteous. If God's blessings can only be secured by Israel's obedience to the law, then the arrival of the kingdom is in jeopardy. Israel's speckled history shows us that the Mosaic covenant must not—cannot—be the final word in God's dealings with humanity.

So God promises through Jeremiah and Ezekiel that he'll do something new. He'll make a new covenant with his people, unlike the covenant he made when he brought Israel out of Egypt and gave them his law. But what makes the new covenant new?

The covenant given at Sinai—often referred to in Scripture as the "old covenant"—could be broken as sinful people rebelled against the Lord, but this new covenant will be unbreakable. It will depend not upon the faithfulness of men in keeping the law, but upon the faithfulness of God. Just as the Lord walked alone in his covenant ritual with Abraham, God alone is responsible for ensuring that his new covenant will accomplish its purpose.

In this new covenant, God declares that he'll change the hearts of his people. Under the Mosaic covenant, it was entirely possible for the majority of people in the covenant community to be dead in their sin and hardened in their rebellion. That's because the law alone has no power to change people—no power to make hearts new. The law can command, but it can't transform.

But God announces that he'll remove the heart of stone—solidified and lifeless in idolatry—and replace it with a heart of flesh that's able to trust and worship the Lord. He'll sprinkle his people with water, cleanse them from their idols, and put a new spirit within them so that they can look to him as the one who satisfies their hearts and is worthy of their praise. God will do what the law alone could not. The law will no longer simply be written on tablets of stone. Now, God's law will be written on the tablets of his people's hearts, a striking metaphor that powerfully demonstrates that God will empower his people to believe and obey his word.

Throughout the Old Testament, as Israel received the just punishment for her continued unfaithfulness, the Lord promised to always preserve a remnant—a collection of people within the larger Israelite community who walked with God in repentance and faith. But when God works to transform the hearts of his people, the covenant community will no longer be a mixed collection where some trust God's promises and others are born into the nation but don't look to him in faith. Under the new covenant, *everyone* in the covenant community will belong to him and know him. The composition and makeup of God's people will be fundamentally altered as all who enter into the new covenant will truly have fellowship with God.

How will the Lord renew his people? "I will put my Spirit within you."[1] The Holy Spirit who anointed prophets, priests, and kings in Israel will now dwell within every believer. The Spirit is the one who will give new life to dead hearts, renewing sinners to fear the Lord and live in covenant with him. God proclaims that through the ministry of his Holy Spirit, he'll cause his people "to walk in my statutes and be careful to obey my rules."[2] The Spirit will make his people spiritually alive and implant God's word in their hearts so that they can trust God's promises, fight against sin, and honor the Lord from grateful, worshiping hearts. So in the new covenant, God will keep his promise to circumcise the hearts of his people,[3] and he'll provide a new power for the life of faith and obedience that the old covenant never offered.

---

1. Ezek 36:27.
2. Ezek 36:27.
3. See Deut 30:6.

But the greatest blessing of the new covenant is contained in these words: "I will forgive their iniquity, and I will remember their sin no more."[4] The law had exposed sin, and the sacrificial system had shown that a substitute would have to bear God's wrath against iniquity. But the chief human problem—the problem of sin—had not yet been decisively answered.

With the new covenant, however, God promises to deal with sin once and for all. No longer will the threats of covenant curses hang over God's people. No longer will God bring judgment and exile in response to unfaithfulness. The Lord will forgive. Sin will be atoned for. And covenant breakers who call upon the Lord will be graciously counted righteous in God's sight.

The new covenant is certainly new, but we need to recognize that it's intimately connected to everything that came before in the Old Testament. Read closely these passages, and you'll hear echoes of earlier promises. The new covenant will overcome the curses of the Mosaic covenant so that sin is forgiven and God's people receive the blessings of the kingdom. It will bring to completion God's covenant with Abraham, for he'll dwell with his people as their God in the place that he gives them. And the restoration that the new covenant ushers in is even pictured as a return to the flourishing and harmony of Eden. The entire tapestry of God's story thus far has been leading to the glory of the new covenant.

But while this new covenant is a precious display of grace for his people, the Lord says that his highest purpose—his primary goal—in making this covenant is *the glory of his name*. Where Israel had profaned his name before the eyes of a watching world, God will now vindicate his holiness. He'll demonstrate that he's the perfectly faithful God, the God worthy of all praise, the God who keeps his promises despite all the sin and brokenness of a tarnished creation. When the Lord pours out his renewing, forgiving grace, the nations will know that he is the Lord. And everyone who receives this extravagant grace from God will gladly turn in worship to glorify his name.

In the pages of the Old Testament, the heights of these new covenant promises are never realized. It's only when a new chapter in God's story opens with the arrival of Jesus Christ that these passages reach their fulfillment. Jesus will bring the forgiveness of God in his death and resurrection for sin. Jesus will establish his new covenant community—the church—and send his Spirit to indwell his people and give them new hearts. Jesus will

---

4. Jer 31:34.

glorify the Father by living the perfectly faithful life and purchasing the redemption God had promised all along. And Jesus will ensure that all of creation is restored from the curse of sin as he guarantees the arrival of the kingdom of God.

*Father, we thank you for the new covenant that you've made with us in Jesus Christ. We've deserved only your wrath, but you've blessed us with grace, granting us forgiveness for our sin, new hearts to love and obey you, and your Holy Spirit to dwell with us. Where we're tempted to be crushed by our failings, comfort us with the assurance that because of Jesus you remember them no more. And as we consider how gracious you are toward us, help our hearts to glorify you by trusting your Son, depending on your mercy, and giving you worship.*

*Part Two*

From the Manger to the (Empty) Tomb

# 16

# The Birth of the King
## *Matthew 1:18–25; John 1:1–18*

THE OLD TESTAMENT TRACES God's story of redemption from creation through the fall and on to his covenants with Noah, Abraham, Moses, and David. God's activity in the Old Testament offers the necessary background, expectations, and categories for understanding how he'll ultimately work to rescue his people from the curse of sin and death. Promises were made, patterns were established, and salvation was foreshadowed, but as the New Testament begins, the time for fulfillment has finally arrived. On its own, the Old Testament is incomplete—a story without a resolution. But the New Testament takes up the narrative of God's rescuing work and shows us what God has done to make good on his word and save his people, and it begins with the birth of the King.

Matthew and John both speak of Jesus' entrance into the world, but they do so from different, complementary perspectives. Matthew focuses on the historical events surrounding Jesus' birth. Mary, betrothed to Joseph, is found to be with child though she's never lain with a man. When Joseph, suspicious of his betrothed, resolves to divorce her quietly, an angel of the Lord tells him that Mary hasn't been unfaithful and that this child has been conceived by the Holy Spirit. The Holy Spirit who hovered over the face of the waters at creation, bringing life to the emptiness, has now brought life to the emptiness of a virgin's womb.

John, on the other hand, says nothing about the specific details of Jesus' birth and instead approaches the coming of Christ from a cosmic perspective. John identifies Jesus as the Word of the Father, the one through whom God spoke all of creation into existence. The Word was *with* God

## Part Two: From the Manger to the (Empty) Tomb

and *was* God. Here's a magnificent biblical insight into the triune God. As the second person of the Trinity, Jesus is God, and at the very same time he's a distinct person along with the Father and Spirit. Into a creation darkened by sin, Jesus comes as the light that reveals God and exposes the hearts of men. And though he'll be rejected by his own people, those who are born of God will receive him and be made children of the Father.

But while Matthew and John have unique focuses, both Gospel writers emphasize a number of very significant themes concerning Jesus' birth.

First, the birth of Christ is the *incarnation of God*. This simply means that God took on humanity. The second person of the Trinity became a living, breathing, growing, hurting human being. He experienced everything that it means to be a human in God's world. Jesus was conceived by the Holy Spirit as confirmation that he is *from* God and that he *is* God. Jesus isn't merely human or merely God. He's the God-man, the incarnate God. "The Word became flesh,"[1] and God lowered himself toward man in grace because man in his creatureliness and sin could never elevate himself toward God.

Second, the birth of Christ is *God dwelling with man.* The incarnation means not only that God has taken on flesh, but that he has made his home in his creation and among his people. Matthew quotes Isaiah 7:14, which was originally spoken to God's people when they were under threat of attack. Through the prophet Isaiah, God promised that a young woman would conceive a child, and this would be a sign that God was with his people to deliver them from their enemies. Isaiah's wife bore a son, and God did indeed deliver them. When Matthew cites Isaiah's prophecy, he's showing us that Jesus expands and fulfills the pattern that was established in Isaiah's day. Isaiah's child was born of a young woman as a sign that God was with them to save them from military enemies, but Jesus is born of a virgin to rescue his people from sin and death as the baby who literally is Immanuel—God with us.

John makes this point when he states that "the Word became flesh and dwelt among us, and we have seen his glory, glory as of the only Son from the Father."[2] In Eden, God walked with Adam and Eve. In the tabernacle, he resided among the wandering nation of Israel. In the temple, he lived in a permanent house at the center of his covenant people. Part of the Lord's covenant promise was that he would dwell with his people as their God,

---

1. John 1:14.
2. John 1:14.

and in Jesus Christ, that promise has become a glorious reality. The Word makes his home in the very creation he called into existence, and Jesus reveals the glory of God to a people who've spent their whole lives reaching for a glory of their own. Jesus is the Temple to whom Solomon's temple pointed, and he dwells with man so that man may eternally dwell with God.

Third, the birth of Christ is a pivotal part of *God's plan of redemption*. The angel of the Lord instructed Joseph to name his Spirit-conceived and virgin-born son Jesus, "for he will save his people from their sins."[3] In Hebrew, this is the same name that was given to Joshua, who delivered Israel into the promised land, and it means "Yahweh saves." So Jesus' very name reveals that he's sent by God to rescue his people from the curse of sin. To spiritual orphans who had rebelled against the Father, Jesus extends the right to be called children of God. This is the essence of salvation: restored fellowship with the living God. The identity of the rescuer foretold in Genesis 3 has now been unveiled. Jesus is the delivering hero of God's story. How he'll in fact accomplish this long-awaited rescue will be uncovered only as the Gospels continue to tell of Jesus' work on earth.

The birth of Christ is a gift of grace, and it's evidence that God is the one who takes the initiative in reconciling sinners to himself. He didn't simply allow sin and death to destroy his creation. He didn't abandon his image bearers to suffocate in their idolatry and alienation. He intervened by sending his Son. Though fallen man could never raise himself to God, God has taken the first step—an infinite leap toward us in Christ.

*Father, we thank you for sending your Son into a sinful world to make sinners into sons. Lord Jesus, we thank you for willingly and obediently entering into your creation to deliver us from the penalty of sin and share your inheritance with us. Holy Spirit, we thank you for conceiving the promised child in the virgin's womb so that God might dwell with man and accomplish our salvation once and for all. When we're tempted to try to elevate ourselves to you with our morality and religiosity and efforts, triune God, comfort us with the truth that you've already descended to us in grace.*

---

3. Matt 1:21.

# 17

# The Water and the Wilderness
## Matthew 3:1—4:11

THIS PASSAGE FORMS A bridge between the narratives of Jesus' infancy and the record of his public teaching and ministry, and with it Matthew provides the lens through which Jesus' words and works have to be interpreted and understood. The accounts of John the Baptist, Jesus' baptism, and the wilderness temptation weave together a staggering number of Old Testament themes that help us grasp Jesus' true significance and make sense of everything he's going to accomplish.

In the Judean wilderness, John the Baptist dresses in camel's hair garments that evoke memories of the prophet Elijah and proclaims that the people of Israel must repent because God's kingdom is at hand. God is preparing to act on the basis of his covenant promises and bring restoration to his creation. As Matthew's reference to Isaiah 40:3 shows, John serves as a precursor to the Messiah, calling the people to confess their sin and baptizing them as a public declaration of their need for cleansing as they await God's nearing deliverance.

Though John baptizes with water for repentance, he points forward to one far greater who will baptize with the Holy Spirit and with fire. Jesus will give the Spirit to everyone who trusts him and will judge all those who reject him with the unquenchable flame of God's wrath. He's going to divide the world based upon their response to him. John exhorts the people of Israel to see the reality of their sin and their need of redemption so that they're ready to receive the Christ when he steps onto the scene. Though the Jewish leaders presume upon their heredity to secure their standing with God, and though we often assume that God will accept us on the basis of some noble characteristic or another, John affirms that there's no substitute for the repentance that acknowledges our guilt before God and looks to him in hope.

Into the Jordan River Jesus wades to be baptized by the prophet. John recognizes that the man approaching him is the Savior he's been announcing and anticipating, and John is understandably hesitant to baptize him. Jesus insists, however, that this is necessary "to fulfill all righteousness."[1] Jesus is God's answer to the world's sin. He has no need of personal repentance because he's not guilty of sin. But one of the ways he exemplifies total human righteousness is by modeling humble submission to God in baptism and identifying with the very people he's been sent to save.

Jesus' baptism is a Trinitarian affair. When Jesus emerges from the waters, the Spirit descends and rests upon him, and God the Father declares with a voice from heaven, "This is my beloved Son, with whom I am well pleased."[2] The Father's words intentionally echo Psalm 2:7 (where the Lord tells his anointed king, "You are my Son; today I have begotten you") and Isaiah 42:1 (where God proclaims, "Behold my servant, whom I uphold, my chosen, in whom my soul delights; I have put my Spirit upon him; he will bring forth justice to the nations"). With one simple sentence, God the Father announces that Jesus is his Son, the Davidic King, and the Spirit-endowed covenant servant who will walk righteously with God and bring God's healing rule to the world. Jesus has been introduced by the Father and anointed by the Spirit, and as he enters his public ministry, everything he does will be accomplished in the power of the Spirit and in joyful submission to the Father.

Having just anointed Jesus at his baptism, the Spirit leads him into the wilderness to be tempted by the devil. Jesus fasts for forty days and nights, is confronted by Satan with a variety of temptations, and faithfully resists in obedience to God as he cites a handful of passages from Deuteronomy. What's fascinating is that each of the passages Jesus references is linked to Israel's wandering in the wilderness after the exodus as they waited to enter the Promised Land. Why would Jesus do that? Why would he intentionally respond to his temptations with allusions to Israel's wilderness journey? He does it to demonstrate that *he's the true Israel.*

Jesus goes into the wilderness just as Israel did. He spends forty days fasting in the place where Israel spent forty years wandering. He's faced

1. Matt 3:15.
2. Matt 3:17.

with temptations to dishonor God that recall Israel's failures to trust, worship, and obey the Lord. But there's one key difference: *Jesus succeeds where Israel failed.* In all of the ways that the nation succumbed to sin in the wilderness, Jesus embodies unrelenting holiness and devotion to the Father. He's the only true covenant keeper who can rightly be called a son of God. And that means that if sinners want to be counted righteous where we've broken God's law, if we want to receive the blessings of God rather than the curses we deserve, we have to hope in the King who kept the covenant as our representative and shares his righteousness with us.

At the water, the Father declared that Jesus is the rescuing Messiah and Spirit-anointed servant. And in the wilderness, Jesus demonstrates that he really is everything the Father said by faithfully obeying in the power of the Spirit. Jesus is bringing God's restoration to humanity by living the obedient human life as a substitute for sinners so that those who come to him in repentance and faith can be given his righteousness and reconciled to God. That's the kind of king Jesus is—the kind of king who willingly walks into the wilderness to face down the devil so that sinners like us can receive grace for all the ways that we've rebelled against God and chased after our temptations. Every other king you serve—whether it's success, approval, beauty, or any other idol—demands that you sacrifice and perform in order to get the good life. But Jesus is the King who sacrifices for us, who performs in our place, who lives as a servant to bring us into the kingdom. You've never met another king like that.

Up to this point in the Gospels, Jesus has hardly uttered a word, and yet the dominant questions that loomed over the story of the Old Testament are beginning to find their answer. Who will be the promised Davidic king? Who will live as the servant of the Lord? Who will embody covenant faithfulness to God where the nation of Israel has repeatedly fallen short? Jesus is the gracious and life-giving answer from God to each of these promises.

*Holy Father, we praise you for the glorious way you've kept your promises of redemption. Thank you for sending Jesus in the power of your Spirit to live in unyielding righteousness so that we could be counted as holy and pleasing in your sight. Give us repentant hearts that readily confess our sin as we look to your grace. Give us comfort in the assurance that your fatherly pleasure is ours. And help us to fight temptation, imitating our Lord, as we worship the one who gave himself for us.*

# 18

# The Ministry of Jesus
## Luke 4:14–44

THE HOLY SPIRIT ANOINTED Jesus at his baptism and led him into the wilderness to face the devil's temptations. Now, Luke tells us that this same Spirit empowers Jesus as he returns to Galilee, a region in the north where his hometown of Nazareth is located. News of Jesus works its way through the countryside, and as the Lord teaches in the Jewish synagogues, the people's response is overwhelmingly positive. This adulation, however, won't last long. As Jesus ministers in the power of the Spirit and further clarifies his identity and intentions, the crowds' initial excitement will progressively turn to something far more sinister and destructive.

In the Nazareth synagogue, Jesus stands to read from the prophet Isaiah and announces the agenda for his entire ministry. Part of Jesus' reading comes from the servant song of Isaiah 61, where the Spirit-anointed servant of the Lord announces that he's been commissioned to proclaim good news to the poor, liberty to the captives, and recovering of sight to the blind as he declares the year of the Lord's favor. According to Leviticus 25, every fiftieth year in Israel was to be a year of jubilee, a year where all the people rested from their labors, indentured servants were freed, and debts were forgiven. Isaiah 61 shows that this year of jubilee was a living picture of the true liberty God would bring his people, a shadow that looked forward to the day when the Lord's anointed would usher in the ultimate freedom and restoration of God's kingdom.

Part Two: From the Manger to the (Empty) Tomb

When Jesus finishes the reading and sits down to teach, he says something incredible: "Today this Scripture has been fulfilled in your hearing."[1] Mincing no words, Jesus tells those gathered in the synagogue that he's the servant of the Lord, anointed by the Holy Spirit to bring about the salvation that Isaiah anticipated. He'll proclaim good news to the poor who recognize their bankruptcy before God. He'll heal bodies that are burdened by the curse of sin and death. He'll free people from their bondage to sin and welcome them into a community where outcasts are adopted as sons and the traditional distinctions of society are no longer permitted to oppress. With every eye in the synagogue fixed on him, Jesus essentially tells them, "Behold your king."

Those gathered in the synagogue respond at first with excitement. The man making all these claims is from their hometown. Surely he'll bring all sorts of prosperity and political benefits to Nazareth! But Jesus challenges their understanding of his mission, offering two examples of prophets from Israel's history who were sent to serve Gentiles. What's his point? Jesus' point is that he hasn't been sent to satisfy Israel's aspirations of power, but to bring all the blessings of fellowship with God to both Jew *and Gentile*. He won't be pigeon-holed by the idolatrous desires of a particular community. He won't be a puppet for anyone else's agenda. Enraged at Jesus' challenge to their expectations, the citizens of Nazareth seek to throw him off a cliff, but Jesus is delivered from them. He won't be overtaken by the crowds until he willingly offers himself up for the forgiveness of sins. But until then, Jesus will continue to provoke the wrath of the spiritually arrogant, the religiously entitled, and the self-righteous with his words and deeds of mercy to unworthy outsiders.

Jesus' pronouncement in Nazareth makes his agenda public, and his ministry in Capernaum begins to enact everything he said he'd do. He teaches with authority and proclaims the good news of God's kingdom. He casts out demons and liberates those who are oppressed by the spiritual forces of darkness. He heals all sorts of diseases and offers restoration to those suffering under the devastating effects of sin on God's creation, and these healings are a foretaste of the freedom from brokenness and death that God's people will one day fully experience. In all these ways, Jesus is waging war against Satan and his oppressive rule over the world by announcing the arrival and demonstrating the power of God's kingdom. Jesus' ministry reveals that the kingdom of God is on the move, bringing

1. Luke 4:21.

life where the kingdom of darkness had only brought bondage. The battle against Satan that began in the wilderness now continues on a new front in the cities of Galilee.

Modern readers frequently find it hard to comprehend why, when casting out demons, Jesus often commands them to be silent. Why does Jesus rebuke these spirits when they rightly acknowledge that he's the "Holy One"[2] and "the Son of God"?[3] But consider who else has attested to Jesus' identity. If you read just the first few chapters of Luke's Gospel, Jesus' identity is confirmed by the angel Gabriel, Simeon and Anna in the temple, and the prophet John the Baptist. The list becomes even more impressive when we consider that God the Father and God the Holy Spirit both validated Jesus as the Messiah at his baptism. Jesus simply has no need of testimony from demonic sources. Plenty of witnesses have testified already, and Jesus' words and works continue to demonstrate that he's the King inaugurating God's kingdom. Where the people of Nazareth balked at the uncomfortable message about Jesus, we need to receive this testimony with open ears and humble hearts, prepared to have our wrong expectations of Jesus' person and mission confronted and shattered by a truth that's so much better.

When the people of Capernaum beg Jesus to stay with them, he offers a significant statement: "I must preach the good news of the kingdom of God to the other towns as well; for I was sent for this purpose."[4] The Father sent the Son in the power of the Spirit to declare to the world the good news that God is overcoming sin, establishing his rule, and welcoming sinners as citizens in his kingdom by grace. The life with God that was fractured by rebellion so long ago is being restored in Jesus, and that message must be proclaimed.

Jesus' ministry is a war against the kingdom of darkness, but the ultimate act of war will only take place when Jesus submits to death at the cross. Precisely when Jesus appears his weakest, he'll powerfully work to ensure the freedom of all who believe. Receiving God's wrath against sin, Jesus will secure the forgiveness necessary for sinners to be made citizens and will strip Satan of his power to accuse and enslave the people of God.

Jesus became a captive to death to set us free for unbreakable life with God. He allowed his body to be broken so that ours could be made new. He received God's fury over our sin so that we could experience the Lord's

---

2. Luke 4:34.
3. Luke 4:41.
4. Luke 4:43.

## Part Two: From the Manger to the (Empty) Tomb

favor. The Messiah King of God's kingdom was exiled from God's presence so that we could be welcomed in to behold his glory. Through Christ, and Christ alone, sinners like us can be restored to God's kingdom family now as we anticipate the day when that kingdom will be brought to completion.

*Holy God, Jesus announces to us that your kingdom has come and shows us in his ministry what your kingdom looks like—freedom, grace, wholeness, restoration, life. Thank you for welcoming us in through the work of your Son. Though we've been liberated from the penalty and power of sin, though we've been reconciled to fellowship with you, we so often revert to our old idols and ways. We try to shape Jesus according to our own agendas rather than submitting to his word. Fix our hearts and hopes on the true Christ so that we might live faithfully as citizens of your kingdom even while we wait for its consummation.*

# 19

# A Blessing and a Prayer

*Matthew 5:1–20; 6:5–15*

THE EARLY PAGES OF the Gospels present us with the clear announcement that Jesus is bringing God's kingdom to the earth. He's restoring the fellowship between God and man that was broken at the fall as he welcomes sinners into life under the saving rule of God. But who gets to be a citizen? How must these citizens live? And how should they address their King? Jesus' Sermon on the Mount, summarized for us in Matthew 5–7, deals with each of these questions as the Lord offers a portrait of his kingdom community.

Jesus' preaching of this sermon from a mountain is no coincidence. *It's a physical clue.* Remember that, after the exodus, Moses journeyed up Mount Sinai to receive God's law and to declare to Israel what it meant to be God's covenant community. Now, Jesus preaches from a mountain as the new Moses: he's creating a new covenant community. But while Moses gave a word of law to Israel, Jesus speaks a word of grace and blessing over all who follow him.

The first portion of Jesus' sermon is a series of blessings commonly called the Beatitudes. The phrase "Blessed are the . . . " is a common one in the Old Testament and is used to describe those who are in right relationship to God and can therefore experience the truly happy life. Jesus' blessings are not commands or prescriptions. They're pronouncements of God's favor, and with them Jesus identifies who's a citizen of God's kingdom and where God's kingdom is already present.

The characterizations of those who have God's blessing—the poor in spirit, those who mourn, the meek—come together to describe people whose only hope is God, who see their spiritual bankruptcy, who repent over their sin, who trust God for their life and righteousness, who've given up on self-sufficiency and thrown themselves on God's mercy, and who walk in faith with the Lord. These citizens are blessed and can rejoice even in the midst of incredibly difficult circumstances not only because the kingdom is theirs in the present, but also because God promises them that in the future they'll be comforted, they'll receive mercy, and they'll even inherit the earth—a magnificent global expansion of God's promise of land to Abraham. The blessed haven't earned the kingdom. Precisely the opposite! They've seen that they couldn't possibly earn the kingdom and by faith have been given the kingdom as a gift of grace.

But how are the citizens of God's kingdom to live in the world? Jesus says his disciples are to be salt and light. That is, they're to have a distinctive flavor to their lives that flows from their trust in and allegiance to Christ as Lord, a flavor that demonstrates the beauty of God's new community in the ways they engage with and bless the world.

And part of the way Christ's disciples live as salt and light is by walking in righteousness according to God's law. Jesus came to fulfill the law. He's the one to whom the law pointed, and he kept the entire law as the perfectly obedient covenant servant. But this doesn't mean that his followers leave God's law behind. On the contrary, Christians are transformed to honor the law in a new way. This is what Jesus means when he says that we must have a righteousness that exceeds that of the scribes and Pharisees. The Jewish leaders in Jesus' day were notorious for obsessing over the external particulars of the law out of self-righteousness while ignoring how God's commands required obedience from a heart of humble dependence and worship. They thought they were keeping the Law, but they were actually flouting it in their pride. Christians must have a different kind of righteousness. All who trust Jesus have been given the righteousness of Christ who kept the law in our place, and we can now seek to worship God by obeying his word from hearts of thanksgiving in humble response to his grace.

The final question Jesus takes up in this passage concerns how citizens of God's kingdom are to address their King in prayer. How are we to commune and fellowship with the God who's rescued us in Christ? Many a well-intentioned Christian has maintained that the child of God can never pray wrongly. But this simply isn't true. Jesus rebukes hypocritical prayer and instructs us about how to approach the Father precisely because it's so *easy* for us to pray wrongly. The prayers of the saints must be responses to what God has first spoken to us in his word, responses that align with his character, works, promises, and revealed will for his people. Jesus' model prayer for his disciples features seven components, each of which informs the way we talk to God as members of his kingdom.

*The address* of the Lord's Prayer calls upon God as "our Father in heaven."[1] Disciples don't merely pray to a far away, disconnected, or impersonal deity. We pray as children to a God who is our loving and gracious Father and who desires to bountifully bless us with good gifts. And he isn't merely *your* Father or *my* Father. He's *our* Father, the head of an entire family, and our prayers should therefore be offered both individually and in community with the church.

*The first petition* is both an acknowledgement of God's glorious name and a request that he would make his name famous throughout the earth. Our posture in prayer must always be one of humble dependence before a holy God, and our chief desire—above everything else—should be that the beautiful God who made us and rescued us through the cross would receive the glory that he deserves. This request will inevitably shape all the others that follow.

*The second petition* asks God to make his kingdom a reality on earth. As the church, we long for God to empower us to live faithfully as citizens of the kingdom here and now, walking in the identity and hope that we've received in Christ. But we also look forward to the day when Jesus returns to fully establish God's reign and make everything new.

*The third petition* is a request for obedience. Just as the angels in heaven joyfully obey the will of the Lord, we want God to be at work among us so that we submit to and live out his will as revealed in Scripture.

*The fourth petition* calls upon our Father to give us what we need each day to live faithfully as his people. We look to God as our sovereign provider with the confidence that even in death, he has provided for us through the resurrection of Jesus Christ.

*The fifth petition* involves regular confession of our continuing sinfulness to God and acknowledgement of our ongoing need for the grace of the cross. When we commune with God, we always approach him as sinners covered by the atoning work of Jesus. And those who've received forgiveness for their sins from God have all the resources necessary to readily and regularly forgive those who sin against them.

---

1. Matt 6:9.

Part Two: From the Manger to the (Empty) Tomb

*The sixth petition* recognizes the ever-present danger of the world around us, the flesh within us, and the devil against us. We beg God to keep us from the grip of temptation and to empower our daily fight against sin so that we can walk in the Christ-exalting holiness that pleases the Father. This is a preparatory prayer that encourages humble self-examination of the patterns of idolatry present in our lives and that grows a deep self-awareness of specific areas where we need God's empowering grace.

Of course, for all the questions about the kingdom that Jesus answers here, one still remains: How can sinners be blessed by God in the first place? As the story of Jesus continues to unfold, we'll see that the blessing of the kingdom can be granted to us only because the King willingly received the curses on our behalf.

*Our Father in heaven, hallowed be your name. Your kingdom come, your will be done, on earth as it is in heaven. Give us this day our daily bread, and forgive us our debts, as we also have forgiven our debtors. And lead us not into temptation, but deliver us from evil.*

# 20

# The Night Meeting

## John 3:1–21

UNDER THE COVER OF darkness, a Pharisee named Nicodemus approaches Jesus. Perhaps this meeting takes place at night because Nicodemus is wary of being seen by his fellow Jewish leaders in the company of a man like Jesus—a man who's made such radical claims about his prominent place in God's redeeming purposes. But this darkness isn't merely physical. It's spiritual, too. Nicodemus recognizes that Jesus must be from God, and his curiosity is piqued, but he still doesn't have eyes to see who Jesus really is. Yet into this darkness, Jesus shines a light that reveals both Nicodemus' (and our) true condition and how God's grand promises find their meaning and fulfillment in his life and, ultimately, his death.

When Nicodemus addresses Jesus as "Rabbi," a gesture of respect, and affirms that God must be with him, we might assume that Jesus would thank him for his politeness and congratulate him for his insight. Instead, Jesus goes straight to the heart of Nicodemus' spiritual need: "Truly, truly, I say to you, unless one is born again he cannot see the kingdom of God."[1] To a respected member of the ruling religious class, Jesus essentially says, "If you're going to lay eyes on God's kingdom, you're going to have to undergo a spiritual transformation so comprehensive that it's like being born all over again."

And Nicodemus completely misses the point. As often happens when Jesus unpacks profound spiritual realities, Nicodemus takes him literally. In a reply that's simultaneously humorous for its absurdity and heartbreaking

---

1. John 3:3.

for its blindness, this Pharisee wonders aloud about the mechanics of a grown man undergoing a second physical birth. "How does that even happen?" he seems to ask.

Ever patient, Jesus clarifies what all this means: "Unless one is born of water and the Spirit, he cannot enter the kingdom of God. That which is born of the flesh is flesh, and that which is born of the Spirit is spirit."[2] To experience physical life, you need a physical birth, but to experience spiritual life, you have to be born of the Spirit. In other words, there's a way to be alive and dead at the same time. There's a way to have a physical heartbeat with no spiritual pulse. And this is the condition that every human being is born into after the fall. We walk in a living death, alienated from and opposed to God, and this death has to be overcome if we're to see God's kingdom and enter in by faith.

Jesus chides Nicodemus. This Jewish leader shouldn't be surprised at what Jesus is teaching. Why? *Because God already said it in the Old Testament.* Back in Ezekiel 36, God promised a new covenant where he would sprinkle his people to make them clean, replace their dead hearts with living ones, and put his Holy Spirit within them. When Jesus says that we must be born of water and the Spirit, he's intentionally drawing our imaginations back to this promise. He's telling us that this new covenant is becoming a reality in him, and in order for us to be part of the kingdom he's bringing—in order for us to be part of God's new covenant community—God has to cleanse us and make us new.

But just as we had no control over when we were born into the world, we have no control over spiritual birth either. Birth is something that is given, not taken. And the Spirit is the giver of this new birth. In both Hebrew and Greek, the same word is used to refer to *Spirit* and *wind*. So Jesus paints us a word picture: the wind blows wherever it wishes, and in the same way, the Spirit is completely sovereign over the new birth. He gives it as a gift of grace where he pleases.

Nicodemus is still incredulous. Jesus has borne witness to what he has seen and heard as the eternal Son of the Father, but Nicodemus (and the rest of a world in rebellion against God) won't receive it. So rather than plumbing the heavenly depths of the Spirit's life giving work, Jesus tells Nicodemus how he, the Christ, will make this new life possible.

2. John 3:5–6.

## The Night Meeting

"As Moses lifted up the serpent in the wilderness, so must the Son of Man be lifted up, that whoever believes in him may have eternal life."[3] Numbers 21:4–9 records a strange event that took place as Israel wandered through the wilderness after the exodus. The people complained against God, so the Lord judged them by sending serpents into the camp, and many people died. But as God judged a rebellious people, he also acted in grace. He commanded Moses to craft a bronze serpent and set it on a pole, and whoever was bitten could look at the serpent on the pole and live. And now Jesus says that all of this points to him.

In the wilderness, a people under God's wrath for their sin could look in faith to God's provision and live. And this is a shadow—a silhouette, an outline—of God's ultimate provision for a dying world. Like the bronze serpent on a pole, Jesus will be lifted up on a cross, and whoever looks to him in faith will be given eternal life. Jesus will take the curse of death so that sinners might receive the gift of life.

At first glance it may seem as if Jesus has offered two competing answers to the kingdom question. You must be born again to live. You must look to Christ to live. But the work of the Son and the work of the Spirit are inseparable. Jesus died so that the Spirit might pour out the gift of life. And when the Spirit makes you new, you can look to Jesus in faith for restoration and life with God. The cross makes the new birth possible, and the new birth directs our hearts to the cross.

And all of this—the work of the Spirit and the work of the Son—flows from the love of the Father. "For God so loved the world, that he gave his only Son, that whoever believes in him should not perish but have eternal life."[4] Don't let the familiarity of that verse dull your heart to its glories. To a world polluted by sin that deserved nothing but judgment, the Father gave his Son so that everyone who trusts the work of the cross could be pulled out from their trajectory of death and be given a life of fellowship with God that begins now and extends through death into eternity.

Jesus' final words here pick up on an important theme from the first chapter of John's Gospel. Jesus' incarnation and entire earthly ministry is a "night meeting" of sorts. The light shines into a world shrouded in darkness, and though people love their darkness and the cover it provides, the darkness has not, *cannot*, overcome the light. But those born of the Spirit allow the light of Christ to expose who they really are, and they walk in

3. John 3:14–15.
4. John 3:16.

repentance so that it's clear to all that their works of faith are a product of God's grace. And so the merciful, faithful, life giving, loving works of the Father, Son, and Holy Spirit redound to the glory of our triune God.

*Loving Father, we praise your name for giving your only Son so that we might have everlasting life in your presence. Exalted Son, we praise your name for entering our darkness and being lifted up on the cross so that we might look to you in faith and live. Sovereign Spirit, we praise your name for granting us the new birth so that we might have hearts that trust and love the Lord. Triune God, help us to walk in your light so that in our faith and obedience your grace is magnified.*

# 21

# The Bread of Life
## *John 6*

AT THIS POINT IN his ministry, Jesus has attracted quite a following. Large crowds have heard about and seen the ways he's healed the sick, so they follow him, probably hoping that one of Jesus' miracles will be directed at them. But Jesus' miraculous deeds aren't just sideshow attractions designed to gather a crowd. In his Gospel, John regularly refers to these works as "signs" because they help reveal who Jesus is and teach about what he's come to accomplish. These signs are a revelation of Christ, and John 6 recounts two such signs that connect Jesus to God's promises in the past so that we might savor him in the present.

The feeding of the five thousand is described in all four Gospels and is for many a fairly familiar episode. But if we're going to truly grasp this event's meaning, we need ears that are primed to hear the echoes of the Old Testament in this account. When the Passover is at hand, Jesus gathers with his disciples on a mountain and miraculously provides bread and fish for an incredible multitude of people. The time (Passover), the place (a mountain), and the act itself (a miraculous provision of food) all recall God's faithfulness in the exodus to deliver and provide for his people through the ministry of Moses.

Upon witnessing this sign, the crowds exclaim, "This is indeed the Prophet who is to come into the world!"[1] Back when Israel was preparing to enter the Promised Land, God promised to one day raise up a prophet like

---

1. John 6:14.

Moses who would speak the word of the Lord to the people.[2] The feeding of the five thousand is Jesus' symbolic declaration that he's the true and better Moses—the one who fills out and completes everything that Moses' ministry anticipated.

The second sign that John records builds on these same Old Testament themes and takes them a step further. The disciples try to cross the sea but fear they won't be able to make it safely to the other side. Just like Israel standing on the shore of the Red Sea, the disciples are afraid they'll be swallowed up by the chaotic waters. When Jesus walks on top of the waves and immediately delivers them to safety, he's not only demonstrating his sovereign power over all the forces of nature. He's identifying himself as *the God of the exodus*—the God who stills the waters for his people.

He comforts his disciples by telling them, "It is I; do not be afraid,"[3] but in Greek the first phrase simply reads, "I am." This is no coincidence. The covenant name that God spoke to Moses from the burning bush is the name that Jesus applies to himself.[4] Yes, he's the true and better Moses, but he's also the God of Moses—the covenant Lord who brings his people on an exodus from sin and death into the salvation of life with God. And when someone like that commits himself in love to you and tells you, "Do not be afraid," his words actually have the power to drive away your fears.

The crowds follow Jesus to the other side of the sea, not because they grasp the true meaning of his signs, but because they know he's able to fill their stomachs and relieve their hunger. But Jesus points them to a deeper hunger and a better bread. There's a spiritual hunger that we can't ignore. God made humanity in his image to experience security, acceptance, and joy in covenant fellowship with him. Our sin broke that fellowship, but the longing—the hunger—remains, and we try to fill our hearts up with the wrong kind of bread: the bread of power, of approval, of control and wealth and pleasure and every other idol.

But Jesus says to our hungry hearts, "I am the bread of life; whoever comes to me shall not hunger, and whoever believes in me shall never thirst."[5] The crowds want Jesus to give them bread like Moses, but he tells them that the Father has given a better bread from heaven that truly gives life to the world—and Jesus is that bread. All of our idols demand that we

---

2. See Deut 18:15–19.
3. John 6:20.
4. See Exod 3:13–14.
5. John 6:35.

work, strive, and labor to find some small relief from our spiritual hunger, but Jesus says the opposite: "This is the work of God, that you believe in him whom he has sent."[6] The bread of life can't be earned. It can only be received as a gracious gift in faith. This is profoundly simple and profoundly difficult all at the same time. All we have to do is trust Jesus. But that means dying to our constant desire to achieve our own salvation and feed our hunger with gods of our own making, and that blessed dying can only happen when the Holy Spirit breathes new life into our hearts and directs us to the cross.

Jesus is the true Moses. Jesus is the covenant Lord. And Jesus is the bread from heaven. This is what the feeding of the five thousand is intended to show us.

Much of what Jesus says in this discourse is perplexing and hard to receive. "All that the Father gives me will come to me, and whoever comes to me I will never cast out."[7] "If anyone eats of this bread, he will live forever. And the bread that I will give for the life of the world is my flesh."[8] "Truly, truly, I say to you, unless you eat the flesh of the Son of Man and drink his blood, you have no life in you. Whoever feeds on my flesh and drinks my blood has eternal life, and I will raise him up on the last day. For my flesh is true food, and my blood is true drink."[9]

Hearing this, many in the crowd turn away. Jesus sees this rejection for what it is, a blindness and opposition to God that can only be overcome by God himself. So Jesus points again to the necessity of the new birth. "It is the Spirit who gives life; the flesh is no help at all . . . This is why I told you that no one can come to me unless it is granted him by the Father."[10]

Turning his attention to the Twelve, the Lord asks if they will walk away too. Peter's answer is as deep and probing as it is straightforward: "Lord, to whom shall we go?"[11] No one else has the words of life. No idol offers the satisfaction, comfort, acceptance, and security—in short, the salvation—that Jesus freely gives to his people through his death and resurrection. This is the sort of question Christians have to learn how to ask when our doubts and lusts tempt us to turn back: Where else could we possibly go? When you've seen Jesus with the eyes of faith, his beauty, supremacy,

6. John 6:29.
7. John 6:37.
8. John 6:51.
9. John 6:54–55.
10. John 6:63, 65.
11. John 6:68.

and grace expose the frailty and ugliness of every other alternative and drive us back to the only one who holds the words of life.

The passage ends with Jesus telling the Twelve that he chose them, even the one who will betray him. Jesus won't be the victim of circumstance. Judas will deceptively hand Jesus over to his death, but Judas only has access to Jesus because the sovereign Lord intentionally brought him into his company. The story of Christ is purposefully and unrelentingly headed to the cross.

*Holy Father, your merciful character and faithful works are infinitely worthy of our praise. You have given us the bread of life, your only Son, so that starving sinners can eat in faith and live. Give us eyes to see Jesus' deeds and ears to hear his words as a revelation of your truth and grace so that we might look to him in hope, have our hunger truly satisfied, and live in the worship and joy of covenant fellowship with you.*

## 22

# The Arrival of the King

## *Luke 19:28—20:8*

IN ONE SENSE, JESUS' entire ministry has been headed toward Jerusalem: "When the days drew near for him to be taken up, he set his face to go to Jerusalem."[1] Jesus came into the world to save sinners, and he presses on to Israel's central city, despite all opposition, to complete the work the Father gave him. On the final journey, Jesus told his disciples, "See, we are going up to Jerusalem, and everything that is written about the Son of Man by the prophets will be accomplished. For he will be delivered over to the Gentiles and will be mocked and shamefully treated and spit upon. And after flogging him, they will kill him, and on the third day he will rise."[2] When Jesus nears the great city, it is with this mission in mind.

On Jerusalem's edge, Jesus sends two disciples into a nearby village to find a colt that has never been ridden. When the colt's owners ask what they're doing, the disciples respond as Jesus instructed, "*The Lord* has need of it,"[3] for Jesus is the covenant Lord, God incarnate. Atop the animal, Jesus rides into Jerusalem, and the multitudes gather around with shouts of praise.

But why would the crowds make such a fuss about one man entering the city, and on a less-than-impressive steed like this one? The answer is found in the promises of the Old Testament. The prophet Zechariah looked forward to the arrival of God's ultimate, anointed king and proclaimed,

---

1. Luke 9:51.
2. Luke 18:31–33.
3. Luke 19:34, emphasis added.

"Rejoice greatly, O daughter of Zion! Shout aloud, O daughter of Jerusalem! Behold, your king is coming to you; righteous and having salvation is he, humble and mounted on a donkey, on a colt, the foal of a donkey."[4] Jesus' entrance into the city on a colt is a symbolic declaration that he is this long anticipated king, bringing salvation with him. We expect a king to approach in royal garb and power, but Jesus comes in humility. We expect a king to arrive mounted on a military horse and poised for war, but Jesus arrives on a donkey, a sign that he comes to bring peace. This King will receive in his body all the violence men can muster so that sinners can have peace with God.

The people of Jerusalem understand the Old Testament significance of Jesus' actions and cry out, "Blessed is the King who comes in the name of the Lord! Peace in heaven and glory in the highest!"[5] The crowds bless Jesus as the coming King, and the Pharisees demand that Jesus rebuke them. Surely the people's words are nothing short of sacrilege! *But Jesus doesn't rebuke them.* He accepts their cries of praise because he really is the King, and he tells the Pharisees that if the people fell silent, then the very rocks under their feet would cry out in worship of the Christ. Of course, it's possible to acknowledge Jesus' identity with much excitement and yet still refuse to trust him, and as the Lord continues to maneuver through his final week, the love of the crowds will quickly grow cold.

When Jesus nears Jerusalem, he weeps. Throughout Israel's history, God anointed prophets to remind the people of their covenant obligations and to warn them of the judgment that would come if they continued in their rebellion. Now Jesus weeps over the city as the prophet to whom all the prophets pointed, and he announces that Jerusalem will be destroyed. The curses of the old covenant included the threat of military occupation at the hands of the nations. As the people had experienced the curses through exile in Babylon, they'll again experience judgment, and this prophetic announcement will be fulfilled when Rome occupies Jerusalem and burns the city to the ground. If Israel won't receive the one who bears the curses of the covenant in place of sinners, then the curses will fall on them. So Jesus weeps over the city. They didn't recognize the God who dwelt among them in grace, so God will come in judgment.

Once inside the city, Jesus enters the temple. The Jewish leaders had allowed an elaborate system of unfair money changing and extortionate

---

4. Zech 9:9.
5. Luke 19:38.

animal sales to grow in the temple court that actually kept people from the presence of God. Jesus' driving out of these oppressive crooks is simultaneously an indictment against the priests of Israel and a symbolic statement that he's the true priest over God's people. Jesus won't profit off of the piety of poor pilgrims. He'll give up everything to ensure that all people can have access to God through him. Jesus is the priest who mediates between God and man. He's the sacrifice who cleanses us so that we can stand in God's presence. And he's the temple in whom we have fellowship with God. But Jesus has challenged the prevailing religious authorities of his day, so the offended leaders seek to protect their power by destroying him.

This is precisely what the chief priests, scribes, and elders are doing when they confront Jesus in the temple. In an attempt to justify their own authority and invalidate Christ's, they ask Jesus who gave him the authority to act like God's prophet, priest, and king. If he says that no one did, they can ignore him. If he says that God did, they'll openly charge him with blasphemy. But Jesus recognizes that this isn't an honest question. No matter what he says, they'll reject him. They're only asking the question to prove their own superiority. So Jesus turns the question back around on them: Who gave John the Baptist his authority? But they can't answer this question without risking their position, so they stay silent, and their cowardice and hypocrisy are exposed. It's not wrong to ask questions about Christ and Christianity—in fact, pressing into your questions is a significant part of the Christian life, one of the profound ways we come to know God and his gospel more fully—but sometimes our questions are little more than a self-justifying mask for our own aspirations of power.

As the Messiah—God's prophet, priest, and king—enters into Jerusalem for the final time, the tone of the story continues to darken. And this darkness will keep creeping across the horizon until it swallows Jesus on the cross.

*Holy Father, we thank you for sending Christ as the humble king who dies to bring peace to his people. We praise you that Jesus is the prophet who speaks and embodies with tearful compassion your word to us. We glorify you because your Son is our perfect priest who cleanses us and invites us to live in communion with you. Help us to daily receive your gospel, treasure your grace, and cherish your presence.*

# 23

# A New Command
## *John 13:1–35*

ON THE LAST NIGHT of his earthly life, Jesus sits down in an upper room for a meal with the twelve and prepares them for his death. John focuses more closely on the events of this particular gathering than any other Gospel writer, devoting four entire chapters to narrating the acts and teachings of Jesus' "farewell discourse." "Now before the Feast of the Passover, when Jesus knew that his hour had come to depart out of this world to the Father, having loved his own who were in the world, he loved them to the end."[1] The love for his people that Jesus demonstrated throughout his ministry extends into the upper room, and his compassionate, sacrificial love will continue—despite opposition, pain, and suffering—all the way to the very end of his mission.

In the middle of dinner, Jesus rises from the table, ties a towel around his waist, and fills up a water basin. Dressed in the garb of a servant, the Messiah washes the feet of his followers. When Jesus arrives at Peter's feet, the disciple will have none of this: "You shall never wash my feet."[2] Peter apparently recognizes how upside-down this situation really is. Peter should be serving the Lord, not the other way around! But Jesus offers a gentle rebuke to this way of thinking: "If I do not wash you, you have no share with me."[3]

---

1. John 13:1.
2. John 13:8.
3. John 13:8.

## A New Command

There's a natural human impulse to prove our worth by offering our service to the Lord, but Jesus says that if we're going to have a share with him—if we're going to be part of his people—*he has to serve us first*. We can't approach God in self-sufficiency as if he needs our service. We have to approach him in a humility that's ready to be served by grace.

Jesus uses this act of foot-washing to teach on a few different levels. In the literal sense, he's simply exercising love toward his disciples by humbling himself as a servant. But this act has symbolic meaning, too. If you're going to belong to Jesus, you have to be served by his death and resurrection. He has to wash your sin in forgiveness as you look to him in faith. When Peter grasps the necessity of being washed by Christ, he's so overcome with zeal that he essentially asks for a bath, but the Lord tells him, "The one who has bathed does not need to wash, except for his feet, but is completely clean."[4] Now teaching at a third level, Jesus applies the image of washing to the practice of lifelong repentance. The one washed by Christ has been made clean once and for all, but we must walk with Jesus in dependence and confession, praying with the Lord's Prayer, "Forgive us our debts."[5]

Having completed his humble task, Jesus encourages his disciples to follow his example. This isn't a command to merely perform foot-washing rituals for one another, but to embrace a whole manner of life where we're regularly humbling ourselves to meet the needs of others. But pay close attention to how Jesus instructs us: "If I then, your Lord and Teacher, have washed your feet, you also ought to wash one another's feet."[6] His work isn't just the model. *It's the motivation, too.* Only when you see that the Lord of glory has served you perfectly and provided for your deepest needs will you be able to lose your protectiveness, embrace self-forgetful meekness, and take on the role of a servant to bless the people around you.

At this point, the mood of the gathering begins to change. In verse 18, Jesus says that Psalm 41:9 ("He who ate my bread has lifted his heel against me") will be fulfilled in him. As the true Davidic King, Jesus must fill out the pattern that David began, and this includes experiencing the sorrow of betrayal at the hands of a friend. Troubled in spirit, Jesus informs the twelve that this betrayal will come from *one of them.*

We may have a hard time believing it, but the disciples don't have a clue which of them Jesus is talking about. Even when Jesus explicitly

---

4. John 13:10.
5. Matt 6:12; cf. Luke 11:4.
6. John 13:14.

identifies his traitor by handing him a piece of bread, the other disciples assume that Judas immediately gets up and leaves so that he can take care of some responsibility associated with his role as keeper of the moneybag. Sin isn't always easily identifiable. A heart devoted to idolatry isn't always observable from the outside. Judas managed to spend years on the inside of the community of disciples without raising a suspicion precisely because wickedness can so easily wear the mask of righteousness. Corruption can adopt the public persona of virtue.

Earlier in the passage, John told us that Satan had already put it into Judas' heart to betray Jesus. But when the Lord hands Judas the morsel of bread, Satan enters into him, animating and empowering his duplicitous actions in an even more influential way.

This is a decisive moment in the Bible's story. The same serpent who deceived Adam and Eve in Eden is coiling for his final venomous strike. Satan will lash out at Jesus' heel, inflicting lethal harm in an effort to destroy the promised Redeemer, but Satan's act of violence will turn back on his own head. Jesus tells Judas, "What you are going to do, do quickly,"[7] demonstrating that he's still in control of everything that's about to unfold. Jesus will only be betrayed because he fully intends to go to the cross.

The wheels of treachery have been set in motion, and Jesus' hour has arrived. In an allusion to Isaiah 49:3, the Lord confirms that he's the covenant servant—the true Israel—who will glorify God and be glorified by God. The Son will glorify the Father by submitting in obedience and worship to death on behalf of sinners, and the Father will glorify the Son by revealing his holy justice and holy love in Jesus' sacrifice at the cross.

The disciples won't be able to follow Jesus where he's going, but they and all those who receive their testimony can live as witnesses to the glory and grace of Christ. And the distinguishing mark of this community of disciples will be love. "A new commandment I give to you, that you love one another: just as I have loved you, you also are to love one another."[8] This command to love showed up in the Mosaic law, but what's new is that Christ's followers are to love *just as he has loved us*. We've seen the extent of God's love in the gospel, and this grace must propel us into a communal life of loving commitment to one another that counters the spirit of the world, points to the kingdom, and testifies that we belong to Jesus.

---

7. John 13:27.
8. John 13:34.

## A New Command

*Father, we bless your name because you've loved us with a perfect love. Give us hearts that rest and rejoice in the sacrificial love of Christ so that we can give ourselves in humble service and love to one another. Work in your church by your Spirit, that the world may see the beauty of life in your kingdom and be drawn to Jesus.*

# 24

# The Father, The Spirit, and the Son
## *John 14*

THE FAREWELL DISCOURSE THAT began with the Lord dressing as a servant to wash his followers' feet now continues with teachings and assurances intended to comfort failing hearts. For the disciples, the ominous prospect of Jesus' betrayal and departure is undoubtedly frightening. Where's he going? Why can't we go with him? Is he abandoning us? What are we to do? But Jesus speaks directly to their fear, and in so doing, he speaks to ours as well: "Let not your hearts be troubled. Believe in God; believe also in me."[1] The Trinitarian promises that follow in John 14 are precisely what disciples need in order to trust God and walk in peace while our Lord is physically absent for a time.

Jesus begins by telling the disciples that his departure has a purpose: he's going to prepare a place for them. Man's descent into sin resulted in expulsion from God's kingdom. The presence of a holy God is hostile territory for those stained with iniquity. But Jesus' departure—by means of his death, resurrection, and ascension—will serve as the once for all sacrifice for sin, covering all who turn to him in repentance and faith, so that we can enter God's presence without being consumed. Jesus prepares the kingdom by making it possible for sinners to have access to God.

Here the Lord makes a staggering claim: "I am the way, and the truth, and the life. No one comes to the Father except through me."[2] We naturally believe—and every other religion teaches—that the way to God is through

---

1. John 14:1.
2. John 14:6.

our moral deeds or our ascent up the ladder of spiritual accomplishment. But the way to God isn't a *what* that you have to perform. It's a *who* that you have to trust. If you want to know the way to God, you must go through Jesus, the "one mediator between God and men."[3] If you want to know the truth of God, you must look to Jesus, who took on flesh to reveal the Father's glory to a rebellious creation. If you want to experience life with God, you must cling by faith to Jesus, who gave up perfect intimacy with the Father and willingly accepted death at the cross to bless his people with everlasting life in covenant with God.

Still not understanding, Philip makes a request: "Lord, show us the Father, and it is enough for us."[4] In one sense, Philip's absolutely right. To behold the Father's glory in fellowship and love is the essence of salvation, and "show us the Father" has been the cry of God's people ever since being banished from the garden. But what Philip misses is that he's beholding the Father's glory at that very moment as he beholds the Son, for the Son is in the Father, and the Father is in the Son. In the mystery of the Trinity, the persons of the triune God are distinct, and yet they're so profoundly one that Jesus can say that they actually dwell within one another. You can't know one person of the Trinity without knowing the others, but you can't know any person of the Trinity without knowing Jesus.

The Lord tells his disciples that they'll not only imitate his works, but those who believe him will do *greater* works because Jesus is going to the Father. This doesn't mean that Christians will perform miracles in greater quantity or with greater significance than Jesus. After all, who among us has fed thousands or risen from the dead to atone for sin? Rather, these greater works refer to the church's ability to point the world to the finished work of the cross in the power of the Spirit. After the Lord dies, rises, and ascends to rule his kingdom from heaven, his followers will be able to testify to the gospel and demonstrate the character of Christ's kingdom with a clarity and power that were previously impossible. And as we witness, Jesus vows that whatever his people ask in his name, he'll do. Whatever we ask on the basis of Christ's work, in line with Christ's character, consistent with Christ's promises, for the glory of Christ's Father, Christ will certainly do for us.

But a very real problem needs to be addressed: if Jesus leaves, even though this brings incredible blessing, his followers have to trod through

---

3. 1 Tim 2:5.
4. John 14:8.

life alone. But Jesus won't leave his people as orphans. He promises that the Father will send another Helper—another advocate, the Holy Spirit, who will graciously work on behalf of sinners like Jesus did throughout his earthly ministry.

And this is for our good. Jesus physically walked with his disciples for a time, but the Spirit will be with his people *forever*. And where Jesus dwelt among men, the Spirit will dwell *within* everyone who trusts the gospel. The Old Testament prophets looked forward to the new covenant promise that God would cleanse his people, give them new hearts, and indwell them by his Spirit. Jesus' teaching in the upper room is a clear announcement that these anticipated blessings are about to become a glorious reality.

Throughout this passage, one prominent refrain keeps on emerging: "If you love me, you will keep my commandments."[5] Obedience is love brought to completion and expressed in life. Sinners who've tasted the covenant love of God in the gospel, and who therefore love Jesus, will demonstrate that love by seeking to honor God and live into his story of the world. Love divorced from obedience is love in name only.

And here, the Spirit is again our Helper. Jesus assures us that the indwelling Spirit will teach us all things and bring to remembrance all that the Lord said. He'll bear witness about and glorify Christ.[6] The Spirit ministers the word of Christ to our hearts, pointing us to the steadfast truth of the gospel and empowering our obedience. The Spirit helps us love and follow our Lord.

Jesus makes one more extraordinary promise to everyone who loves him and keeps his word: "my Father will love him, and we will come to him and make our home with him."[7] If you're in covenant with God through living faith in Christ, you have the love of the Father. And the Father and the Son will make their home with you. How? Through the ministry of the Holy Spirit. In a very real sense, the Father and Son are present with you by the Spirit. The persons of the Trinity enjoy loving fellowship with one another, but through the gospel, they share that fellowship with us and pull undeserving sinners into their covenant life of joy.

How can God's children have peace while Christ is absent for a time? We have to see that Jesus has granted us the ultimate peace—peace with

---

5. John 14:15; cf. vv. 21, 23–24.
6. See John 15:26; 16:24.
7. John 14:23.

## The Father, The Spirit, and the Son

the triune God. "Peace I leave with you; my peace I give to you."[8] The Son shows us the Father and gives us access to his presence. The Spirit dwells within us, ministers to us the word of the Son, and gives us a foretaste of the Trinitarian fellowship that we'll enjoy forever in God's restored creation. So while we may feel alone, we are most assuredly not alone. So let not your hearts be troubled, and neither let them be afraid.

*Most gracious Father, thank you for loving us in Christ in spite of our sin. Most holy Son, thank you for taking the cross to prepare a place for us in your kingdom. Most merciful Spirit, thank you for making your home in us and working in us the faith and obedience that are pleasing in the sight of our covenant God. Calm our fearful hearts as we hold onto these precious promises. Triune God, we bless your name.*

---

8. John 14:27.

# 25

# The High Priestly Prayer
## *John 17*

CHRIST'S MOST EXTENDED PRAYER recorded in the Gospels is found here in John 17. This conversation with the Father is known as Jesus' "high priestly prayer" because it's primarily the Lord's intercession on behalf of his people. Like the Israelite high priests under the old covenant who would enter God's presence as representatives of the people, Jesus goes before the Father to make requests for his church. Jesus permits us to eavesdrop into the intimate communion of God the Son with God the Father so that we might know what our Lord desires for his kingdom people as we live between his cross and his second coming. This prayer is rich, but a few themes consistently emerge.

## The Glory of the Triune God

From the first syllables of Genesis, everything that God's been doing has been aimed at manifesting the glory of the Trinity. As the hour of his death draws near, Jesus prays that this ultimate purpose will be fulfilled and that God will be glorified in what's about to take place. The Son possessed glory with the Father before the beginning of time and set it aside to take on flesh according to the Father's will. Throughout his life, Jesus glorified the Father by walking in trust, worship, and obedience, accomplishing the work the Father gave him. Now he makes a request: "Glorify your Son that the Son may glorify you."[1]

---
1. John 17:1.

Jesus asks the Father to demonstrate the beauty of the Son in his atoning sacrifice for sin. The darkest moment in history will be the moment when Christ's glory is most wondrously revealed. And as the Father glorifies the Son by working salvation through his death, the Son will glorify the Father by walking in perfectly faithful obedience and bringing sinners back into covenant fellowship with God. The Father makes the Son the object of saving faith. The Son restores all who believe to life with the Father. And thus the persons of the Trinity glorify one another in redemption.

But the end of the prayer reveals that Jesus doesn't merely want to *show* God's glory. He wants to *share* it. Jesus revealed the glory of the Father in his life that we might walk in his character. He makes his people participants in his glory through his death and resurrection. And he prays that his church may one day join him in the presence of the Father to spend eternity beholding the joy-inducing glory of Christ.

## The Preservation of the Church

Trusting God and living accordingly in a fallen world is hard. No one knows that better than Jesus. He was hated because he didn't conform to the God-rejecting, man-exalting ways of the world, and he recognizes that his church will experience this same hatred as they follow their Lord. Jesus guarded his followers while he walked with them, but since he's departing, he asks the Father to keep them in his name, to preserve them in faith in the midst of threat and hardship.

In every time and place, Christians face social pressure and persecution—sometimes subtle, sometimes violent—and these can bring powerful temptations to abandon the path of discipleship. Jesus could've prayed for the Father to pull his people out and keep them safe from the temptations and dangers of being outsiders, but instead, he prays for their sanctification, for their holiness, for God to keep them holding firmly to his promises as they live among the very people who are likely to despise them.

But at work underneath the world's opposition is one whom Jesus elsewhere calls "the ruler of this world"[2]—Satan. That's why the Lord also prays that his church would be kept from the evil one. From the garden to the cross, Satan battled against God and his people, and he continues to fight in spite of the fact that Jesus has sealed his defeat. Still, anyone who's faced down a wounded animal knows that the creature only gets more dan-

---

2. John 12:31; 14:30.

gerous as it gets more desperate. So Jesus prays, knowing that the predator will keep hunting God's people in an effort to destroy their faith.

## The Unity of the Church

Every Christian is united by faith to Jesus through the work of the Spirit. But believers are also united to one another. When sinners repent and trust Jesus, we're brought into one family with one gospel under one Father through the sacrifice of one Son and the ministry of one Spirit. The gospel takes all kinds of people and binds them into one covenant body in submission to one Lord, so Jesus prays that this unity would be expressed in the life of the church. To be one doesn't mean that Christians must never disagree on certain issues or that every church must be formally connected to all the others. It means that we already possess an unbreakable union in the Spirit and that we must therefore relate to all the parts of Christ's body with the humility and love that's fitting for a family.

This unity is connected to the other two themes of Jesus' prayer. The Lord says to the Father, "The glory that you have given me I have given to them, that they may be one even as we are one."[3] He has revealed his glory to the church so that we might reflect the character and unity of our triune God. And he pleads, "Holy Father, keep them in your name . . . that they may be one."[4] Jesus prays for our preservation in the faith so that we'll be of one mind around the gospel and so that we'll be able to love one another in the midst of our very real differences.

And this sort of gospel empowered unity will be a testimony to the world of the truth and power of Christ. The very shape of the church's life together will witness to the kingdom. All sorts of boundary markers separate people in the world: race, class, sex, culture. But the church is the one community where those differences, while still present, don't have the power to divide. The gospel overcomes every natural boundary to make one people in Jesus, and when the church embodies that oneness in the ways we relate to our brothers and sisters in the Lord, people will see that there's something truly and distinctly powerful about the good news of Christ.

But how do we know God will answer this prayer? We know that he'll bring us to himself to behold his glory because he glorified his Son when Jesus died to make us his own. We know that he'll preserve us in grace

3. John 17:22.
4. John 17:11.

because Christ already purchased us at the cross and has given us his Spirit, so not even Satan himself can pluck us out of God's hand. We know that he'll make his church one because we *are* one in Jesus, and the Spirit that ties us together will keep working to help us witness to the unity and love of the kingdom. So the church can live in the confidence that the Lord who prayed for us on his final night secured God's answer to his prayers at the cross and now lives in the presence of the Father to intercede on our behalf, ever praying that the vision of John 17 would be a reality in our lives.

*Father, we thank you for sending us a merciful and compassionate mediator who graciously pleads on our behalf. Glorify yourself in our faith and obedience as we enjoy you now and look forward to delighting in your glory forever. Keep us standing firm in the gospel so that we can resist the seductive temptations of the world and the evil one. And because your church is one in Jesus, help us to live as one in a manner that points others to your kingdom.*

# 26

# The Table of the Lord

## *Mark 14:10–25*

John's Gospel spends multiple chapters recounting Jesus' works and teachings in the upper room on the night before his crucifixion, but while the other Gospel writers devote far less space to this particular setting, they focus much more attention on the meal that Christ shares with his disciples. Mark's account of Jesus' institution of the Lord's Table may be brief, but this meal offers us a lens for understanding what's about to happen at the cross and is loaded with significance for Christ's church as we keep on participating in this meal together.

From the start of Jesus' ministry, the religious leaders have been outraged by his message of grace for the unworthy and his rebukes of their spiritual pride. Jesus is a threat to their prominent position, and he must be stopped. But in an ironic twist, the same fear of man that has fueled the leaders' hatred of Jesus has also prevented them from destroying him. The crowds have flocked to Jesus, and if the chief priests openly oppose him, they risk losing the favor of the people.[1] And so the fear of man leaves them paralyzed. In order to look good, they must kill Jesus. In order to look good, they can't kill Jesus—at least not yet.

When Judas enters the picture, however, everything changes. Judas has access to Jesus and, for a small price, he can deliver him into their hands under the cover of night. Here is a horrific marriage of idols. If the religious leaders will feed Judas' greed with silver, he will feed their fear of man by

---

1. See Mark 14:1–2.

helping exterminate the one obstacle to their public praise. So together they plot to kill the Son of God.

Mark points out that Jesus gathers to celebrate the Passover with his disciples "on the first day of Unleavened Bread, when they sacrificed the Passover Lamb."[2] Every year, families in Israel would gather to celebrate God's deliverance of his people from slavery in Egypt. A lamb was slain, and the family shared the Passover meal to remember God's faithfulness. But Jesus isn't just participating in the Passover. *He's fulfilling it.*

The Passover celebrated Israel's exodus from Egypt under the leadership of the prophet Moses. But Jesus is the better Moses who leads his people on a better exodus. When the Lord instructs two of the disciples to prepare a place to dine in the city and foretells what they'll find, he's not performing a parlor trick. He's confirming to them that he's a prophet—*the* prophet—sent from God to lead his people to freedom. Moses spoke the word of God and brought his people from political slavery into freedom. Jesus *is* the Word of God, and he'll rescue his people from the slavery underneath every slavery—our spiritual slavery to sin and death.

During supper, Jesus reveals that one of his followers will betray him and offers a very interesting explanation: "For the Son of Man goes as it is written of him."[3] The seed of the woman must be struck by the serpent's fang. The Messiah must, like David, suffer before entering his glory. The servant must be pierced for our transgressions and crushed for our iniquities in order to bless us with peace, present an offering for guilt, and make many to be accounted righteous. Submitting to this betrayal, Jesus is self-consciously bringing the story of God to its climactic point.

As Jesus celebrates the Passover, he uses the meal to teach about his approaching death, and he packs the celebration with new meaning. Taking the bread and wine, Jesus says to his followers, "This is my body . . . This is my blood of the covenant, which is poured out for many."[4] The covenant that Jesus is referring to is the new covenant, the covenant that God promised he would one day make with his people to cover their sin completely by grace. Jesus acts as the Lord of the covenant—the giver of the covenant—and announces that God is keeping his promise, accomplishing their forgiveness, and granting them life. Jesus is establishing a new way of relating to God.

2. Mark 14:12.
3. Mark 14:21.
4. Mark 14:22, 24.

## Part Two: From the Manger to the (Empty) Tomb

But the covenant Lord is also the sacrificial lamb. Jesus sets the terms for our covenant relationship with God, and he does it by laying down his life as the sacrifice for sin. In Egypt, the Israelites smeared the blood of a lamb over their doors so that God's judgment would pass them by. Now, on the day when the Passover lamb is sacrificed, Jesus proclaims that his body and blood will be given to cover his people because he's the final Passover Lamb whose sacrifice protects repentant sinners from the judgment of God.

In the ancient world, the institution of a covenant was always accompanied by a ratification ceremony to both symbolize and confirm the new relationship. So when Jesus announces the new covenant, he gives his disciples a meal that serves as both a sign and seal of his gracious gospel. As a sign, the bread and wine are visible and dramatic portrayals of Jesus' work at the cross where he gives himself, body and blood, for our salvation. As a seal, the Lord's Table marks out those who belong to Jesus by faith and confirms to us that we have fellowship with God and that his promises are for all who trust him. That's why Jesus instructs his disciples, "Do this in remembrance of me."[5] As long as the church lives, our practice of the Lord's Table is a visible proclamation of the gospel and a confirmation of God's covenant with us.

There's one more dimension of the Table that we shouldn't ignore. After sharing the meal, Jesus says, "Truly, I say to you, I will not drink again of the fruit of the vine until that day when I drink it new in the kingdom of God."[6] Jesus' covenant feast with his disciples anticipates the joyous banquet that we'll celebrate with him when he returns to restore creation and when the Lord "will swallow up death forever."[7] So the Lord's Table looks back to the cross, offers nourishment for the present, and points forward to God's glorious future.

Every time the church practices the Lord's Table, we're signing the gospel, putting it on display in bread and wine. We're sealing the new covenant in Christ's blood, receiving God's testimony that he is ours and declaring in response that we are his. We're fellowshipping with the God who gives himself to us in grace and with the people of God who are bound to us by the Holy Spirit. And we're joyfully looking toward the day when we'll feast in the physical presence of our risen and reigning King.

---

5. Luke 22:19.
6. Mark 14:25.
7. Isa 25:8.

## The Table of the Lord

*Father, you've lowered yourself to us in so many ways. You gave us your will in Scripture in words that we can understand. You sent your Son in our flesh to show us your glory and purchase our redemption. And you've granted us a meal to direct our hearts to the gospel and nourish us with the promise that all who trust Jesus are irrevocably and eternally yours. For all these things, we bless your holy name.*

# 27

# In the Garden of Anguish
## *Matthew 26:30–56*

THE STORY OF THE Bible began in the garden of the Lord, the first expression of God's kingdom in his creation. In that blessed garden, Adam disobeyed God, and the kingdom of life, fellowship, wholeness, worship, and joy was broken by sin. Now, Jesus kneels to pray in a different garden—a darker garden—as he prepares to obey his Father's will in the face of agonizing circumstances. And by his obedience, he'll overcome the disobedience of Adam and Adam's children, and he'll restore God's kingdom so that sinners can once again dwell in the presence of their Lord.

After singing a hymn and rising from dinner, Jesus takes the eleven remaining disciples to the Mount of Olives and makes an ominous prediction: "You will all fall away because of me this night."[1] Jesus isn't prognosticating an unforeseeable event. He's simply applying the Scriptures. The prophet Zechariah wrote, "'Awake, O sword, against my shepherd, against the man who stands next to me,' declares the LORD of hosts. 'Strike the shepherd, and the sheep will be scattered.'"[2] Jesus has already taught that he's the Good Shepherd who lays down his life for his sheep,[3] but now he confirms that God himself will be the one who strikes him down and that this will result in a time of great confusion and trial for the disciples.

Peter responds to Jesus with a startling level of self-confidence. Everyone else may fall away, but not him—not a chance! Of course, Peter's

---

1. Matt 26:31.
2. Zech 13:7.
3. See John 10:11–18.

confidence is misplaced, and this kind of misplaced confidence is little more than arrogance, bravado, pride. *And it's deadly.* When you can't fathom the prospect of failure and fail to see how fragile you really are, that's precisely the point when you're most vulnerable to temptation. If you see your weakness and your need of God's grace, you'll have a profound self-awareness that knows your limits, looks to Christ, and guards you from foolishness and sin. But if you're blinded by your pride and walk in smug self-assurance, you'll scoff at the prospect of temptation, but only until that temptation unexpectedly ensnares you—just as it will Peter when he fulfills Jesus' words.[4]

On the Mount of Olives, Jesus leads his disciples to a garden called Gethsemane. Jesus says with a troubled spirit, "My soul is very sorrowful, even to death."[5] His disciples would've certainly recognized echoes of the Psalms in his words. Psalm 42:5 cries, "My soul is cast down within me." And in Psalm 22:15, David laments to the Lord, "You lay me in the dust of death." In his life, Jesus experienced the whole range of human emotions. He knows what it's like to bear a sadness so severe that it feels like living death. When Jesus cries out to God in the garden, he shows us not only that there are times when we can cry as Christians, but that there are times in a distorted, fragmented, broken world when we *must* cry. But Jesus isn't just another sufferer. He's the ultimate sufferer. He's the man of sorrows whose righteousness deserves perfect joy but who walks into the darkness of God's wrath for sinners. That's why Jesus' soul is sorrowful, and that's why, even in your deepest sadness, you need never despair. You can cry with God in faith that Jesus is with you in the valley because he already went through the valley for you.

The Lord asks the eleven to pray, and he moves a bit farther into the garden, falling to his face and asking, "My Father, if it be possible, let this cup pass from me."[6] The Old Testament often used the cup of God's wrath as a metaphor for God's holy fury against sinful rebellion. This is the cup the Father has given the Son, and Jesus pleads that, if there's any other way to accomplish salvation, God would spare him from tasting it. But in the midst of sorrow and fear, Jesus perfectly submits in faith: "Nevertheless, not as I will, but as you will . . . My Father, if this cannot pass unless I drink it,

---

4. See Matt 26:69–75.
5. Matt 26:38.
6. Matt 26:39.

your will be done."⁷ Jesus is willing to obey the Father even to death, and he'll drain the cup of God's wrath all the way down so that his people can drink their fill from the overflowing cup of God's blessing.

Jesus repeatedly returns to his disciples to find them tapering off to sleep. Rebuking them, he instructs them to pray that they might not give in to temptation, but they fail to grasp the seriousness of what this means, so they doze again. In the garden, both the disciples and Jesus demonstrate weakness—but completely different kinds of weakness.

The disciples are weak because they think they're strong when they're not. Theirs is a foolish weakness that underestimates the power of temptation and the danger of sin. Jesus, on the other hand, is weak because he refuses to trust his own strength and instead submits to the Father's will and depends upon the Spirit. His is a godly weakness that models the self-denying path of faith and obedience. Ironically, the disciples' apparent strength is actually perilous weakness, but Jesus' apparent weakness is in fact the truest kind of strength, because humble dependence will empower him to walk the road the Father has set before him.

Judas enters the garden of prayer, much like the serpent entered the garden of fellowship long ago, and he brings an armed multitude, hoping to take Jesus captive. With a word of respect and a sign of friendship—a kiss—the betrayer signals to the crowd that Jesus is the target of their bloodthirsty hunt. When the people seize the Lord, one of the disciples unsheathes his sword and strikes.⁸ But Jesus instructs him to stand down and offers three reasons for refusing violence:

1. Violence is the way of death, an endless and ever intensifying cycle of destruction: "All who take the sword will perish by the sword."⁹

2. Should he choose to, Jesus is perfectly capable of defending himself: "Do you think that I cannot appeal to my Father, and he will at once send me more than twelve legions of angels?"¹⁰

3. The promises of God in Scripture must be fulfilled in the death of Christ. Peter may believe that he's saving his Lord from death, but the Lord must die to save Peter from death.

---

7. Matt 26:39, 42.
8. John 18:10–11 tells us that this disciple, rather unsurprisingly, is Peter.
9. Matt 26:52.
10. Matt 26:53.

## In the Garden of Anguish

Jesus won't take up the sword. He won't make any more appeals for divine deliverance. He won't sidestep his appointed end. The Son has submitted to the Father. He'll accomplish salvation. And he'll respond with faith and peace even in the face of direct attack. With the assurance that Jesus' death secures their life, his disciples must likewise take up their cross, be willing to suffer in peace and love for their enemies, and follow after the Lord.

The passage's final sentence hangs like a dark cloud: "Then all the disciples left him and fled."[11] Where Jesus is going, he must now go alone.

*Father, our spirits are willing, but our flesh is often so very weak. Help us see ourselves soberly and rightly so that we'll depend on your grace and provision instead of our stubborn and feeble strength. We thank you that you didn't remove the cup of wrath from Jesus and that he willingly drank it all so that we could drink from the cup of blessing. In this confidence, give us the strength to follow after Jesus, leaving behind the way of the sword, and submitting in glad faith to the way of the cross.*

---

11. Matt 26:56.

# 28

# The Court of Injustice
## *John 18:28—19:16a*

ONCE ARRESTED, JESUS IS brought before the high priest and the whole Jewish council to be questioned about his teachings. Is he really the Christ? Does he really claim to be the Son of God? The leaders of Israel have been plotting Jesus' destruction for quite some time, and now they seize their opportunity to get rid of him for good. But while their proceedings may have the appearance of justice, it's only a facade, because there's no justice to be found in the trial of the Lord.

The council sends Jesus from the high priest's home to the headquarters of Pilate, the governor and representative of Rome's authority in Jerusalem. Here, the leaders' hypocrisy is on full display. They refuse to enter Pilate's headquarters in order to remain ceremonially clean for the Passover feast, but they're dedicated to annihilating the very one to whom the feast points. They'll eat their meal with meticulous care once they've slaughtered the Son like an innocent lamb.

Similarly, the council recognizes that Roman law doesn't permit them to exercise capital punishment. They wouldn't dare kill Jesus themselves, but they have no problem coercing Pilate to do their lethal bidding. In the religious leaders, we see a lip-service to the law (both God's and Rome's) that in reality dishonors the law at every turn. But their petition of Pilate, intended to discredit and destroy Jesus, will only further validate his claims to be the Son of God. As John points out, the preferred Roman method of execution—crucifixion—will fulfill Jesus' predictions of his death in a startlingly literal manner: "As Moses lifted up the serpent in the wilderness, so must the Son of Man be lifted up."[1]

The sole motivation of the scribes, priests, and Pharisees is the preservation of their power, and Pilate proves to have the same agenda. He initially asks Jesus if he's the King of the Jews, or more plainly, "Are you a political threat to me and to Caesar?" Jesus' answer reveals that he *is* a king, but not the kind of king Pilate is expecting: "My kingdom is not of this world."[2]

Jesus hasn't come to immediately set up a physical kingdom with national borders and armed defenses, and his people aren't violent militants aiming to overthrow existing political rulers. Jesus has come to welcome sinners into a spiritual kingdom of peace and fellowship with God as his citizens continue to live in all the kingdoms of the world, but in a new way—a way defined by the gospel. And he'll establish this kingdom not through acts of raw power and domination, but through his humility, weakness, grace, and death. The kingdom of God isn't like the kingdom of Rome because King Jesus isn't like King Caesar.

The Lord presses deeper and tells Pilate that his purpose for entering the world is to bear witness to the truth. Jesus entered into a creation blinded and deceived by sin to reveal the life giving truth and glory of God. Those who are of the truth—who believe the truth and belong to the Christ who is the truth—listen to Jesus' voice and live under his kingship.

But Pilate is completely uninterested in this sort of talk. He dismisses Jesus' claims with a single question: "What is truth?"[3] Pilate has power, and power always gives us the impression that we can create the truth rather than submit to it. Power makes us drunk with self-sufficiency, magnifies our blindness, and can easily fool us into believing that we have no need of God's unsettling, liberating, subversive, redemptive word. The serpent deceived Adam and Eve with the promise of power, and humanity has been living in that deception ever since.

Pilate's lack of concern for the truth leads to a lack of concern for justice. He tells the crowd of Jews, "I find no guilt in him,"[4] but his devotion to power—his *idolatry* of power—makes him unwilling to take decisive action to ensure that Jesus is treated like the innocent man he is. The governor appeals to the Jewish custom of releasing a prisoner at Passover, but the

---

1. John 3:14.
2. John 18:36.
3. John 18:38.
4. John 18:38.

crowd opts instead for a convicted robber, murderer, and insurrectionist. Irony abounds yet again. Barabbas (whose name means "son of the father") really is a violent threat to Rome, but the true Son of the Father, who taught his followers to render unto Caesar what is Caesar's,[5] will be eliminated as a political threat.

Hoping to appease the people, Pilate has Jesus flogged and publicly humiliated. But the appetite for violence hasn't been satisfied. Instead, the chief priests lead the call for Jesus to be crucified and argue that he's guilty of blasphemy. So long as Jesus draws breath, he remains a threat to their idols, and he must therefore be exterminated. And we protect our idols in the same way. Perhaps we don't resort to physical violence all that often, but the relational violence of harsh words, manipulation, shaming, and passive-aggressive behavior are incredibly destructive, too. The road of idolatry is littered with the carcasses of innocent people who got in the way.

"When Pilate heard this statement, he was even more afraid,"[6] not because he cares about Jewish blasphemy, but because religious unrest in his province could reflect poorly on his leadership and jeopardize his status. The governor tries to interrogate him one last time, but Jesus remains silent, embodying the words of Isaiah 53:7: "Like a lamb that is led to the slaughter, and like a sheep that before its shearers is silent, so he opened not his mouth." Offended at this silence, Pilate proudly asserts that he holds Jesus' fate in his hands. But, in a difficult statement, the Lord reminds Pilate that he only holds authority in this situation because God has sovereignly brought Jesus before him. On top of that, Caiaphas—who concocted this plan and delivered Jesus to the governor—has been controlling Pilate like a pawn from the beginning. Jesus challenges Pilate's arrogance by pointing out that he's not even the primary *human* agent in the events leading to the cross. Pilate is subject to God's sovereign control of history, and his thirst for power makes him vulnerable to coercion from others.

When Pilate continues to bargain for Jesus' release, the leaders change tactics. The threat of religious unrest didn't work, so they turn to political manipulation: if Pilate frees an opposing king, he makes himself an enemy of Caesar. The priests reject Jesus and affirm that they have no king but Caesar. They've accused Jesus of blasphemy, but in their pandering to Roman power, they've committed blasphemy themselves, denying God's authority as their sovereign King and laboring to murder the Messiah. This

---

5. See Matt 22:15–22; Mark 12:13–17; Luke 20:19–26.
6. John 19:8.

time, their threats hit the mark, and Pilate's idolatrous hunger to maintain power outweighs any desire for justice. So at right about the time when the Passover lambs would be slain, he delivers the Lamb of God to be crucified.

Jesus doesn't deserve to die, but he willingly becomes a victim of the systems of self-preservation and power at work in the world and in so doing exposes their ugliness, wickedness, and bankruptcy. He suffers terrible injustice on the way to the cross, which means that he can compassionately sympathize with those who suffer unjustly. And as the righteous substitute, he'll satisfy God's perfect justice when he gets to the cross, which means there's hope for all of us who are guilty of violently pursuing our idols at the expense of God and others.

*Holy Father, we're so often tempted to follow after the way of the world and sacrifice truth, love, and justice for the sake of power, self-protection, and glory. As we behold our King and see the injustice he received in order to reconcile us to you, would you comfort us in our afflictions, forgive us for our participation in oppression, and grant us the strength to resist the temptations of power and the courage to hold fast to the soul-satisfying truth of Christ.*

# 29

# The Cross

*Mark 15:16–47*

AT JESUS' BIRTH, GABRIEL announced that Mary's son would save his people from their sin, and in his ministry, the Lord intentionally set his face to go to Jerusalem in full knowledge that he'd be crucified. So Jesus' whole life has been leading here. The Old Testament exposed humanity's sin and looked forward to God's work of restoration. So the whole Bible has been leading here. At the outer edges of eternity past, the triune God purposed to glorify himself through the Father's sending of the Son in the power of the Spirit. So all of history has been leading here. As Jesus is paraded down the road to Golgotha and nailed to a cross in shame, the story of God is reaching its long anticipated culmination. And in the span of a mere six hours, everything will change, because Jesus is securing and fulfilling every promise that God's ever made.

Leading Jesus away from Pilate's headquarters, a whole battalion of soldiers dresses the Lord in purple, crowns him with thorns, and mocks him as the King of the Jews. But they're completely unaware that the title they hurl as an insult is the title Jesus actually deserves. Jesus *is* the King of the Jews. He *is* the Messiah, sent by the Father as God's answer to his covenant with David. And while we rightly recoil at the soldiers' ignorant barbarity, a crown of thorns is fitting headwear for the King who will bear the curse of sin that lingers over every part of creation.

We might expect Mark to shock us with the gory details of Roman execution, but he spends less than one sentence on the act itself: "And they crucified him . . . "[1] Mark's goal isn't to give us a horrifying description of the crucifixion. His goal is to reveal the *meaning* of crucifixion. The details he includes are historically true—they actually happened—but they're intended to echo Old Testament promises and patterns that clue us in to the significance of the cross.

The soldiers divide Jesus' garments and cast lots to see who gets what piece of clothing, mirroring the account of King David's suffering in Psalm 22:18. The Lord is offered wine mixed with myrrh, reminiscent of the sour wine David received in Psalm 69:21. And Mark specifically notes that passersby "derided him, wagging their heads,"[2] connecting Jesus' suffering to the head-wagging scorn David experienced in Psalm 22:7. Throughout the Psalms, David emerges as a model of intensely personal and unjust suffering. So when Mark repeatedly references David's Psalms, he's showing us that Jesus is the better David. David was a righteous royal sufferer, and Jesus is the perfectly righteous royal sufferer. He's the King who lived in spotless obedience before the Father, and he's receiving a death he's done nothing to deserve.

Jesus is crucified alongside two robbers, one on his right and one on his left, and this simple detail carries tremendous biblical import. Isaiah wrote that the suffering servant of the Lord would be "numbered with the transgressors,"[3] bear the sin of many, and intercede on behalf of guilty people. By recording that Jesus was literally placed among thieves, Mark's inviting us to see that Jesus is Isaiah's suffering servant and that his death is the atoning sacrifice that heals our spiritual wounds, cleanses our filthiness, and brings us peace with God.

The chief priests and scribes call out in mockery, "He saved others; he cannot save himself. Let the Christ, the King of Israel, come down now from the cross that we may see and believe."[4] In their minds, a true king would aim his power at self-preservation and avoid the suffering of the cross. Jesus' claims to save others must therefore be false if he can't even save himself. But in God's wisdom, it's precisely in refusing to save himself that Jesus saves others. In God's wisdom, it's precisely in remaining nailed to the cross that Jesus demonstrates the glories of his kingship.

---

1. Mark 15:24.
2. Mark 15:29.
3. Isa 53:12.
4. Mark 15:31–32.

Part Two: From the Manger to the (Empty) Tomb

From about noon to three, darkness shrouds the whole land. In the Old Testament, darkness often signified God's judgment, as in the plague of darkness that covered Egypt. And it was frequently used to describe the "day of the Lord"—the day when God would pour out his holy wrath on human sin. When God darkens the sky over the cross, he's confirming to the whole world that his judgment is being poured out on his Son, that the day of the Lord has broken into history and is happening on Jesus' shoulders.

Jesus cries out in anguish from the cross the first verse of Psalm 22, "My God, my God, why have you forsaken me?"[5] King David initially prayed those words because it felt like God had abandoned him. Jesus prays those words because God really has abandoned him. Where the Father had eternally looked upon his Son with nothing but divine pleasure and love, he now looks upon him with all the anger that sin deserves. And as Jesus breathes his last, the temple curtain that separated God's dwelling place from the outside world is torn *from top to bottom*. God reaches into his creation and opens the way for sinners to enter his presence through the atoning work of Christ.

A Roman centurion, who'd undoubtedly seen innumerable brutal executions before, nevertheless sees that there's something different about Jesus' death. God's grace pierces a soldier who likely had a hand in piercing Jesus, and he offers the confession of every sinner who becomes a disciple: "Truly this man was the Son of God!"[6] This Gentile's words give us expert testimony that Jesus' death isn't just any normal death, and they show us that God's promise to Abraham—that the nations would be blessed through him—is being fulfilled in Abraham's greater son.

A number of women look on from a distance, and a member of the Jewish council named Joseph of Arimathea wraps Jesus' lifeless body in a linen shroud, buries the corpse in his personal tomb, and rolls a stone over the entrance in the presence of witnesses so that no one can get in—or out. Why does Mark tell us all this? The reason is simple: he's confirming on the authority of multiple eyewitnesses that Jesus is really dead. People watched him perish, prepared his body for burial, and saw the stone close off the tomb. When odd reports begin circulating that Jesus is in fact alive, no one will be able to reasonably claim that it's because he never died.

Though a number of players have contributed to Jesus' murder, the person ultimately responsible for the cross is none other than God himself.

---

5. Mark 15:34.
6. Mark 15:39.

Satan entered Judas and empowered his lustful betrayal. Judas delivered the Lord to the religious leaders for silver. An angry mob went out with swords and clubs to arrest Jesus in the night. The community called for blood. Pilate handed Jesus over to be crucified. Disciples scattered, soldiers struck, and onlookers gave their tacit approval with shaking heads and deriding words. But in all of this, God has been the primary actor. He has sovereignly used Satan's sin and the world's violence to work his promised salvation through the death of his Son.

At the cross, Jesus took the darkness of God's wrath so that you could live with the light of God's face shining on you. He was forsaken by God and exiled from his presence so that you could have access to the Father as his covenant child. He hung upon the tree of death so that you could take and eat from the tree of life, restored to fellowship with the triune God. Cling to Jesus' death by faith and live.

*Father, in the cross you punished your Son with everything that we deserve so that you might eternally bless us with everything that he deserves. He took on physical death and spiritual condemnation so that we could know everlasting life and gracious acceptance in covenant with you. By your Spirit, help us to live in the comfort, peace, security, and joy that the cross offers, knowing that every one of your promises to us has been decisively and gloriously kept.*

# 30

# The Empty Tomb
## *Luke 24:1–35*

On the Sunday after Jesus' crucifixion, a group of women journey early in the morning toward the tomb, burial spices in hand. The Lord had on multiple occasions predicted that he'd be delivered to men, killed, and raised on the third day, but his followers aren't eagerly anticipating resurrection. They go to the tomb expecting to find a dead man.

Their reaction may seem hard for us to understand, but remember what they must've been thinking. Jesus had claimed to be the Messiah who was restoring and ushering in the kingdom of God. But when Jesus was nailed to the cross, it really looked like the King had been defeated and the kingdom destroyed. Everyone knows that a dead Messiah is no Messiah at all, so the only thing left to do is to take the burial spices to the tomb and weep.

But what they find there changes everything. Perplexed by the empty tomb, the women are confronted by two angelic messengers who call them to remember the promises Jesus made while he was still with them. The women quickly return to tell the disciples that Christ has risen from the dead, but the group shrugs off the unbelievable report as an idle tale born from grief and an overactive imagination. Peter, however, runs to the tomb and, spying the empty linen cloths, marvels.

The women proclaim and Peter marvels because a dead man is alive again, but what's the significance of Christ's resurrection? If a dead king is

## The Empty Tomb

a failure, what does it mean if "he is not here, but has risen"?[1] It means that Jesus isn't a failure at all.

In the trial leading up to his death, Jesus was maligned and accused, and the cross was a public declaration that Jesus stood under the curse and judgment of God. The resurrection, however, is Jesus' vindication—God's declaration that Jesus is in fact the perfectly righteous covenant keeper. The guilty verdict pronounced over Jesus at the cross is reversed when the resurrection announces that Jesus is innocent of every charge leveled against him and holy in God's sight.

The empty tomb demonstrates that Jesus walked into death and received the curse not because he was guilty of sin, but because he was offering himself as the only acceptable substitute for sinners. Jesus took the death that we deserved at the cross so that we could share in the life that he deserved by his resurrection. When Jesus walked out of the grave, he turned the curse of death backwards so that everyone who's united to him by faith can have life and fellowship with God. And if Jesus is the truly righteous and royal Son of God who couldn't be held by death, then that means that everything he ever claimed about himself is true. It means he really is the king, redeemer, rescuer, and hero of God's story—he really is *God*—and you've got to trust his work and submit to his lordship.

Later that day, two disciples walk along the road to Emmaus. As they talk with one another, no doubt trying to understand how everything could go so wrong, the resurrected Lord joins them on the road, but their eyes are kept from recognizing him. Jesus asks what they're talking about, and the two stop in their tracks, their faces clouded with sadness. They can't believe this fellow hasn't heard about what happened in Jerusalem, so they recount the events concerning Jesus of Nazareth. They tell him about Jesus' mighty words and deeds, but when they speak of the crucifixion, they offer a revealing admission: "But we had hoped that he was the one to redeem Israel."[2] They *had* hoped, but that hope died with Jesus, and now there's only disappointment.

Of course, in this moment Jesus could've simply shown them the marks in his hands and feet to prove that he'd been raised from the dead, but instead, he takes them back to God's word. "'Was it not necessary that the Christ should suffer these things and enter into his glory?' And beginning

---

1. Luke 24:6.
2. Luke 24:21.

with Moses and all the Prophets, he interpreted to them in all the Scriptures the things concerning himself."[3]

Jesus shows them that they're wrong about the crucifixion because they're wrong about the Bible. These two disciples were expecting a king who would sweep in with unmistakable power and usher in the kingdom by reestablishing Israel's political dominance on the world stage. So Jesus walks through all the Scriptures, demonstrating how the story of God has been leading *first* to the Messiah's redemptive suffering, and only then to his glory.

The promised deliverer had to be struck on the heel before decisively crushing the serpent's head. The anticipated Davidic king had to suffer like David before taking David's throne. The servant of the Lord had to pour out his soul to death and be numbered with the transgressors before being highly exalted and prolonging his days. The whole Bible has been preaching that King Jesus will restore God's kingdom by identifying with sinners and laying down his life in our place. The suffering precedes the glory.

Why have we labored to see how the story of the word at every point directs our focus to the Lord Jesus? *Because that's how Jesus understood the Bible.* And during the forty days between his resurrection and his ascension, that's how he taught his disciples to understand the Bible, too. The rest of the New Testament will give us a glimpse into what the resurrected Lord must've shown his followers when "he interpreted to them in all the Scriptures the things concerning himself."[4]

It's important for us to recognize that Luke presents Christ's resurrection not as myth or allegory or fable, but as historical fact. And if we consider his account carefully, we'll find that the details ring true. Luke includes the names of multiple eyewitnesses whom his earliest readers could seek out to corroborate his story. He tells us the first witnesses of the empty tomb were women, whose testimony wouldn't even be admissible in court. He recalls how the disciples responded not with courage and faith, but with skepticism and disappointment. And his central point is that a man has risen from the dead, something completely foreign to both Jewish and Greek sensibilities. The concept of resurrection doesn't fit into the modern naturalistic worldview, and it didn't into the first century worldview either.[5]

---

3. Luke 24:26–27.

4. Luke 24:27

5. Greek philosophy elevated the spirit over the body, so the concept of a physical resurrection that restored the material body would've been seen as both undesirable and

## The Empty Tomb

If Luke were trying to get a new religion off the ground by propagating a lie, these are the precise things he *wouldn't* do. The only reason to tell the story this way is because that's how it actually happened.

If Jesus didn't rise from the dead, then he's just another figure on the pages of history. But if the tomb is really empty, then he's the very center and meaning of history, the fulfillment of God's story, and the hope of salvation, righteousness, and life for all who believe. As the disciples proclaimed to one another, "The Lord has risen indeed!"[6]

*Holy Father, we thank you for raising Jesus from the dead by the power of your Spirit. You showed him to be the righteous Son of God, and by his resurrection he defeated sin and death so that we could enjoy a never-ending life of fellowship with you. As we cling to the hope of Christ's sacrificial death and glorious resurrection, give us hearts that worship his name and submit to his lordship in security, confidence, and joy.*

---

ridiculous (see Acts 17:32). While the Jews believed in a resurrection at the end of the age, there was no expectation of a single individual being raised from the dead in the middle of history. So the resurrection of Christ pushed against the expectations of both worldviews.

6. Luke 24:34.

# Interlude

*And beginning with Moses and all the Prophets, he interpreted to them in all the Scriptures the things concerning himself.*

Luke 24:27

In a confrontation with the Jewish leaders earlier in his ministry, Jesus made a startling proclamation: "You search the Scriptures because you think that in them you have eternal life; and *it is they that bear witness about me*, yet you refuse to come to me that you may have life . . . If you believed Moses, you would believe me; *for he wrote of me.*"[1] When he'd risen from the dead, he showed the disciples on the Emmaus road how the whole Old Testament points to him. And around a meal of broiled fish, he taught the gathered disciples, "These are my words that I spoke to you while I was still with you, that everything written about me in the Law of Moses and the Prophets and the Psalms must be fulfilled,"[2] and he opened their minds to finally understand what the Scriptures are all about.

The Gospel writers never recount for us what Jesus specifically told his followers when he taught them how to read the Bible through the lens of the cross—as the story of God that culminates in Jesus' life, death, and resurrection. But they don't really have to, because their very way of telling the story of Jesus clues us in to so many of the beautiful ways in which he fulfills the Scriptures. In other words, what they learned from Jesus is woven into

1. John 5:39–40, 46, emphasis added.
2. Luke 24:44.

## INTERLUDE

the narratives of the Gospels themselves and shapes how the New Testament authors understand and speak about Jesus' identity and work.

So how does Jesus fulfill the Scriptures? Here are just a few of the answers the New Testament offers for us to meditate upon, celebrate, and look to for comfort and hope.

- Adam, as the head of humanity, disobeyed God in the garden and was cast into the wilderness, meriting the covenant curse of death for all who are in him. Jesus, as the head of a new humanity, obeyed God in the wilderness to bring us back into the garden city of God's presence, bearing the curse of death and meriting life for all who are in him by faith.
- A deliverer was promised who, though struck by the serpent, would crush the serpent's head. Jesus, though led to the cross by Satan's schemes, defeated the devil through his sacrificial death for sin.
- Noah brought his family safely through the flood of God's judgment on the ark. Jesus brought his family safely through the flood of God's judgment at the cross.
- Abraham was promised that he and his offspring would be a blessing to all the nations of the world. Jesus, the ultimate offspring of Abraham, welcomes all the nations of the world into the blessing of salvation.
- Moses spoke God's word of law to the people and led them on an exodus from slavery into freedom. Jesus spoke God's word of blessing to the people and led them on an exodus from bondage to sin and death into liberty and life with God.
- The Passover lamb was slain, and its blood marked the Israelites' homes so that God's judgment would pass them over. Jesus willingly poured out his blood as a covering for sin so that God's judgment would pass over all who trust him.
- God's law commanded total righteousness, promising blessing for obedience and threatening his covenant curse for disobedience. Jesus obeyed the law as the perfect law keeper, meriting the blessings and bearing the covenant curse in the place of law breakers.
- Joshua led Israel in battle to bring them into the Promised Land of rest with God. Jesus waged war against Satan to bring his people into

## Part Two: From the Manger to the (Empty) Tomb

the true Promised Land of eternal life and rest with God in a renewed creation.

- David suffered unjustly but was vindicated and promised a royal dynasty that would reign forever. Jesus suffered the ultimate injustice in the cross but was vindicated in the resurrection so that he might reign forever as king.

- Solomon feared the Lord and grew in wisdom, and he was honored as the wisest man alive before descending into foolishness. Jesus is the Lord we are to fear in order to grow in wisdom, and as the incarnate Wisdom of God, he lived the flawlessly wise life as a substitute for fools.

- The temple was the dwelling place of God's presence among the people where sacrifices were made to atone for sin. Jesus took on flesh to dwell as God among his people, and he offered himself as the final sacrifice to atone for sin.

- Israel was cast into exile because of her disobedience against God. Jesus experienced the ultimate exile at the cross to bring sinners back into fellowship with God.

- Elijah healed the sick and raised the dead. Jesus healed the sick and raised the dead, and then rose from the dead himself in order to secure healing and resurrection for his people.

- Isaiah predicted a suffering servant who would bear the sins of the people before being exalted to glory. Jesus lived as the suffering servant who was crushed for our iniquities before being exalted in his resurrection.

- Jeremiah wept over Judah as he prophesied judgment against their rejection of God. Jesus wept over Jerusalem as he pronounced God's judgment against their rejection of him, the Messiah.

- Ezekiel anticipated a new covenant where God would cleanse his people from sin and put his Spirit within them. Jesus sealed the new covenant when he died for the forgiveness of sins and sent the Holy Spirit to dwell within all who believe.

- Esther entered the presence of the king, willing to lose her life to intercede for her people. Jesus entered his creation, knowing he'd lose his life to intercede for his people.

## Interlude

- The prophets spoke God's word to the people. Jesus lived as the incarnate Word of God, revealing the glory of God in grace and truth.
- The priests mediated between God and the people, offering sacrifices for sins. Jesus offered himself as the sacrifice for sin and now mediates for his people in the presence of the Father as our great high priest.
- The kings were called to rule as sons of God who imitated and reflected his kingship over his people, but they often led the nation into disobedience and idolatry. Jesus lived as the true Son of God and rose from the dead as the victorious and righteous King, and he now rules over his kingdom people from heaven in holiness, grace, and glory.

And this is just the beginning. May God open our minds to understand and cultivate our hearts to receive the story of the word as the story of Jesus.

*Part Three*

From Christ's Ascension to Christ's Return

# 31

# The Commission

*Matthew 28:16–20*

IN ONE SENSE, THE whole Bible is about God's mission. The triune God formed image bearers who could see, savor, and reflect his glory as they lived in community with him in his world. When his image bearers rebelled, he took the initiative to make a covenant promise to restore his kingdom and extend blessing to the ends of the earth. And at just the right time, the second person of the Trinity—the Son of God himself—took on humanity and entered into the hostile territory of his darkened creation to redeem a people for himself.

At every step in the story of the word, God has been on mission. He's been working according to his sovereign purpose to craft a kingdom community who will magnify his beauty in worship by finding its highest joy in fellowship with him. And at every step, he has invited his people to take part in his kingdom mission. Adam and Eve were called to fill the earth and subdue it as God's image bearers. Israel was to live as a kingdom of priests, revealing God's character and word to the nations. But now that Jesus has accomplished salvation through his death and resurrection, he invites his followers to participate in the God glorifying mission of God in a new way. As the Father sent the Son into the world, so now the Son sends his people into the world as witnesses of God's grace in Jesus.

On a mountain in Galilee, the eleven disciples—with hosts of other disciples likely joining them—gather to behold the risen Christ. When they see Jesus, many of them begin to worship him. This detail is easy to pass by, but it's incredibly significant. Every good Jew knew that worship was to be directed to God alone. Offering worship to a human being would've been

## Part Three: From Christ's Ascension to Christ's Return

blasphemy. But immediately following the resurrection, the thoroughly Jewish disciples bow down in worship to Jesus. *And Jesus accepts their worship.* If the disciples had any doubt during his earthly ministry, the resurrection serves as conclusive proof that Jesus, while fully human, is the fully divine Son of God. Any man who can bear death as a substitute for sinners and overcome death in resurrection life is no mere man. He's God, and he's worthy of our worship.

The resurrection was the Father's declaration that Jesus is Lord and King, and Christ tells his disciples, "All authority in heaven and on earth has been given to me."[1] With this statement, Jesus draws an intentional connection to the Old Testament. The prophet Daniel experienced a vision in which "one like a son of man"[2] approached God. "And to him was given dominion and glory and a kingdom, that all peoples, nations, and languages should serve him; his dominion is an everlasting dominion, which shall not pass away, and his kingdom one that shall not be destroyed."[3] When Jesus proclaims that all authority is his, he's saying that he's the anticipated eternal King who rules over an eternal kingdom and that people from every nation will be brought under his gracious rule.

As the King, Jesus commissions his disciples to go into the world as ambassadors of the kingdom and "make disciples of all nations,"[4] and this commission is the continuation of what God has been doing with humanity from the beginning. Back in the book of Genesis, God made a covenant with Abraham, promising him that all the families of the earth would be blessed in him. Jesus, the true seed of Abraham, bore the curse of sin so that every kind of person could be reconciled to God by faith in Christ. And now, the disciples are to take the good news of Jesus' finished work to the nations so that all peoples might experience the blessing that God promised and Jesus purchased. Jesus fulfilled the Abrahamic covenant, and the Great Commission is a call to announce this to the world.

But Jesus doesn't merely tell his followers to go. He doesn't leave the details up to them. Jesus tells them *how* to go, *how* to make disciples. And his instructions are really quite simple: baptize and teach.

The command to baptize in the name of the triune God reveals that the task of discipleship—the task of the Great Commission—is fundamentally

1. Matt 28:18.
2. Dan 7:13.
3. Dan 7:14.
4. Matt 28:19.

communal. Baptism signals one's entry into the church. It's a communal ceremony that visibly proclaims the death and resurrection of Jesus, declares the believer's union with Christ by faith, and welcomes the believer into the new covenant community. And it's God's way of marking out who belongs to him. God set his name on Israel to mark them as his covenant people,[5] and when Christians are baptized into the name of the Father, Son, and Holy Spirit, God is announcing that he's given his family name to them in the gospel so that the world will know that they belong to him. So the task of making disciples first requires bringing repentant sinners into the fellowship of the church through baptism.

But discipleship is more than believing the gospel, receiving forgiveness, and being baptized. Discipleship is a whole life of growing up into the identity that's been given to us. It's a lifelong process of learning to live under the gracious lordship of Christ. That's why Jesus calls his followers to make disciples by teaching them to observe all his commands.

Through the ministry of the word, God exposes our remaining sin, nourishes us with his gospel, and calls us to obedience to his holy law. This kind of teaching takes place in the corporate worship of the church, but it also happens in the informal moments of community life—as we have conversations with believers, pray with fellow Christians, and observe the lives of other disciples that model for us what it looks like to follow Jesus in faith. And as God's word touches every part of who we are, we grow to observe his commands in gratitude and humble obedience, and the church's life points to the character of Christ's kingdom.

So Jesus' commission is a commission for the church. It's a call for the church to multiply, to baptize repentant sinners into the community, and to apply God's whole word to the whole life of every disciple. It's a commission for the church to live as the covenant family of God in every context, ministering in word and sacrament while faithfully proclaiming and demonstrating the kingdom in our life together. That's how disciples grow up into maturity, and that's how the world will hear and see what God's kingdom is all about.

This is a high calling, but Jesus empowers the church's perseverance in discipleship by bookending his commission with two glorious promises. On the front end, he announces his sovereign kingship over all things. In other words, he's in complete control, and as Daniel's vision makes clear, people from every tribe, nation, and tongue *will* be brought into his

---

5. See Num 6:22–27.

## Part Three: From Christ's Ascension to Christ's Return

kingdom. Because Jesus is the authoritative Lord, the church goes out in mission with the confidence that Christ's purposes will come to pass.

And on the back end, Jesus assures us, "I am with you always, to the end of the age."[6] Though the resurrected Lord will ascend to his place at the right hand of the Father, he vows to nevertheless be present with his people wherever they go until the day he returns to renew his entire creation and reign in glory. Jesus will send another advocate, his Holy Spirit, to dwell with and within his covenant people. So no matter the opposition she may face, the church is never alone—never abandoned—as she goes about the ordinary kingdom business of making disciples. And that is a precious promise, indeed.

*Father, we thank you for crowning Jesus as Lord of all, and we thank you for bringing us into his kingdom by faith. As we rejoice in Christ's sovereign lordship and enjoy the empowering presence of your Spirit, help us—together with the community of saints—to make disciples of the nations according to Christ's command. Let those who are far from you be brought near through the witness of your church, and grow us all into maturity that we might proclaim and demonstrate your kingdom, living as your redeemed family here on earth.*

---

6. Matt 28:20.

# 32

# The Ascension of the King

## *Acts 1:1–11*

ON THE SUNDAY BEFORE Passover, Jesus entered Jerusalem riding on a donkey and was eagerly welcomed by the crowds as they shouted, "Blessed is the King who comes in the name of the Lord!"[1] On Friday, Christ revealed the glories of his kingship in the ugliness of the cross. Wearing a crown of thorns, the King received the curse of death so that his people could receive the kingdom. Though to the world the crucifixion may have seemed like an invalidation of Jesus' kingly claims, God offered his glorious perspective in the resurrection. The Father vindicated his Son and proclaimed that Jesus is indeed the righteous Lord and rightful King by raising him from the dead. And now that the King has been coronated and presented in splendor, it's time for him to take his throne.

Over the course of forty days following his resurrection, Jesus appeared to his followers and offered them physical proof of his victory over death. Luke includes this to emphasize once again that Jesus really did accomplish something in history. The essence of most religions is good advice that tells you what you need to do so that you can get to God. But the essence of Christianity is the good *news* that Jesus did what you couldn't do in order to bring you to God. The gospel isn't a set of instructions or an abstract philosophy of life. It's the announcement that something actually happened: in Jesus Christ, God accomplished the salvation we desperately need. Jesus really lived. He really died. And he really rose again. The whole fabric of Christian hope hangs on the fact that Jesus got up out of the tomb

---

1. Luke 19:38, citing Ps 118:26.

## Part Three: From Christ's Ascension to Christ's Return

on that first Easter morning. That's why Luke is so diligent to remind us that people saw the resurrected Lord.

While he was with them, Jesus also taught the apostles about the kingdom of God. The term "apostle" refers to those eyewitnesses of Jesus who were commissioned by their Lord to provide authoritative testimony to the world concerning his life, death, and resurrection. The teachings of the apostles in Acts and the rest of the New Testament aren't the private interpretations of select individuals. They're the teachings of men who saw, touched, and heard Jesus before and even *after* his resurrection. If the apostles learned about the kingdom from the King himself, we can confidently accept their testimony.

After meeting their risen King and receiving his teaching about his kingdom—how he's fulfilling God's promise to restore sinful, broken people to total peace with God—the disciples ask, "Lord, will you at this time restore the kingdom to Israel?"[2] And Jesus' answer is *yes*. They can't know the precise timeline of how the kingdom will progress and be brought to completion, but Jesus really is restoring the kingdom of God.

In order to do justice to Jesus' answer, we have to revisit what the Old Testament envisioned when it looked forward to the restoration of God's kingdom. The Lord promised that he would pour out his Holy Spirit on his people. He'd make his people witnesses who would declare his glory. He'd heal the divisions in Israel and unify his kingdom under the Messiah King from David's line. And he'd even bring the nations into his kingdom—into all the blessings of belonging to God—as full citizens and members.[3]

With those promises in mind, we can rightly hear what Jesus says: "But you will receive power when the Holy Spirit has come upon you, and you will be my witnesses in Jerusalem and in all Judea and Samaria, and to the end of the earth."[4] He'll send the Spirit to empower his disciples as witnesses, and as the gospel goes forth, not only will Judea and Samaria (the divided southern and northern kingdoms of Israel) be brought together under Christ, but peoples from the ends of the earth will be welcomed into the kingdom as well. Jesus' answer reveals that everything the Old Testament promised about the restoration of the kingdom is coming true in him,

---

2. Acts 1:6.

3. See, for example, Joel 2:28–32; Isa 32:15–17; 43:12; 44:3–5; 49:5–6; Ezekiel 37:15–28.

4. Acts 1:8.

## The Ascension of the King

and his disciples get to participate in the expansion of his kingdom as the gospel multiplies in the world.

But Jesus' kingdom doesn't arrive all at once. One of the huge themes of the New Testament is that the kingdom of God is both *already here* and *not yet complete*. Jesus currently reigns over a spiritual kingdom of grace. Believers are citizens and truly have fellowship with God, but the blessings of the kingdom must be experienced by faith as the Lord continues to welcome sinners in by his gospel. But one day, Christ will return to judge sin, restore his whole creation, and reign over a physical kingdom of glory. When that day comes, all the blessings that Christians presently enjoy by faith will be tangible realities as we dwell face-to-face with God in his redeemed world.

Every other kingdom expands through military might and coercive power, but that's not how Jesus grows his kingdom. God's kingdom expands as the Spirit empowers the church to faithfully proclaim the gospel and demonstrate the character of the kingdom in her life. The nations will be reconciled to God—rebels will be made citizens—as Jesus' disciples announce and live into the reality that Christ has dealt with sin and as sinners trust and submit to the lordship of Christ.

Upon saying these things, Jesus is lifted up and taken out of their sight. But Christ's ascension is more than a mere change in elevation. As a king ascends his throne, Jesus ascends to take his position of royal authority at the right hand of God the Father. And that's profoundly good news for his people.

Christ's ascension is a physical demonstration of his kingly power over all things. As Paul says, the Father "raised him from the dead and seated him at his right hand in the heavenly places, far above all rule and authority and power and dominion, and above every name that is named, not only in this age but also in the one to come."[5] Jesus exercises sovereign control over all things, working for the glory of God and the good of his people even in the opposition we face and the suffering we experience.

And the ascension means that "we have an advocate with the Father, Jesus Christ the righteous,"[6] one who mediates as our great high priest before the face of God. Jesus offered himself as the atoning sacrifice for our sin at the cross, and he now stands in God's presence, pointing to himself

---

5. Eph 1:20–21.
6. 1 John 2:1.

## Part Three: From Christ's Ascension to Christ's Return

as our covering and interceding for us in prayer.[7] The precious benefits of Christ's ascension have the power to drive away our fears and embolden our witness.

As the disciples gaze into heaven, two angels testify that Jesus will come back in the same way he left. So while the ascension confirms to us that Jesus is physically absent for a time, it also directs our hearts to the promise that he'll physically return to make all things new and bring his glorious kingdom to completion.

Luke says that his Gospel only dealt with "all that Jesus *began* to do and teach."[8] The book of Acts is the account of what Jesus *continues* to do and teach as he reigns over his kingdom from heaven and as his Holy Spirit works in and through his church. But for now, the apostles must remain in Jerusalem and wait for the promised Spirit to arrive.

*Our Father, we thank you that Jesus Christ has ascended his throne to rule over all things from heaven and intercede in your presence as our gracious priest. Guard us from the temptations of glory and domination that lead us to treat Christ's kingdom like the kingdoms of the world. As we rest in Jesus' sovereign authority and atoning work, and as we look forward to the day when he'll return in glory, empower us by your Spirit to live faithfully as citizens of your kingdom and to proclaim the gospel to all peoples.*

---

7. See Heb 7:25.
8. Acts 1:1, emphasis added.

# 33

# The Sending of the Spirit

*Acts 2:1–41*

Now ten days removed from Christ's ascension, the whole group of disciples gathers together in Jerusalem. Without warning, something like a gusting wind rushes through the house where they're meeting, and "divided tongues as of fire"[1] appear and rest on each of them. The storm of God's presence rushes but doesn't destroy. The fire of God's presence descends but doesn't consume. Jesus was destroyed and consumed by God's holy presence at the cross so that God could be present with his people in grace. In this mysterious moment, the Holy Spirit fills the disciples and miraculously enables them to speak in other languages. Jesus had promised to send the Holy Spirit to empower his church's witness in the world, and on the day of Pentecost, the ascended Lord keeps his word.

Pious Jews from "every nation under heaven"[2] are in Jerusalem during this time, and they gather around to see what all the commotion is about. To their astonishment, these foreigners hear the disciples preaching about God's mighty works in Jesus in their native tongues. The restoration of Israel is beginning as scattered Jews from all over the world are united by faith under Christ's kingship, and soon this restoration will extend to Gentiles as well.

At Babel, God judged and restrained rebellion by confusing languages and dividing the people.[3] At Pentecost, God forgives rebellion by using the

---

1. Acts 2:3.
2. Acts 2:5.
3. See Gen 11:1–9.

various languages of the world to bring people together in Jesus. The effects of sin are being undone as the Spirit goes forth with the gospel of God's grace in Christ.

This multinational collection, perplexed by these strange events, asks precisely the right question: *What does this mean?* Scoffing onlookers suggest that the disciples may have broken into the wine cellar a bit early, but Peter, once too afraid to even acknowledge Christ, lifts his voice to answer.

Just a few short weeks ago, Peter was nowhere to be found as his Shepherd was struck, and now he boldly speaks the gospel to the very sorts of people who called for the Lord to be crucified. This dramatic shift in Peter—and a similar change among all the apostles—is inexplicable, unless of course he really met the risen Christ. The only way a coward like Peter can become a herald who's willing to risk rejection—and even his life—for the sake of the gospel is to be utterly convinced that his message is true.

The Jewish audience entered Pentecost assuming the truthfulness and authority of the Old Testament, so that's where Peter begins. Recognizing his context, he takes the Scriptures his hearers already believe and shows how they point to Jesus as the fulfillment of all God's promises. And in the process, he gives us a marvelous example of how the apostles understood the Old Testament as finding its ultimate meaning in Christ.

Peter starts by citing Joel 2:28–32, where the prophet looked forward to the last days when God would grant the blessings of the new covenant and pour out his Holy Spirit on every one of his people. No longer will the Spirit only dwell upon special, anointed leaders. He'll be with and within young and old, men and women, slave and free, *every* member of the covenant community. The God who was present in Eden, in the temple, and in Christ will now be present by his indwelling Spirit.

Peter's point is that the last days Joel anticipated have finally arrived, and the Spirit he longed for has been given. The "wonders in the heavens above and signs on the earth below"[4] signal the arrival of the day of the Lord, God's intervention in history for judgment and salvation. Interestingly, these wonders and signs match many of the descriptions surrounding Jesus' death, resurrection, and ascension. Why? Because the day of the Lord happened at the cross where God judged sin and worked salvation for his people. And now in these last days, every person who calls on the name of Christ in faith will be blessed with the Spirit, reconciled to God, and delivered.

---

4. Acts 2:19, citing Joel 2:30.

## The Sending of the Spirit

Peter continues with a clear announcement of the gospel: Jesus of Nazareth was crucified and killed by men according to the sovereign plan of God, and he was raised from the dead because death couldn't keep him. Since death is part of God's curse on sin, it can only stake a claim on sinners. But God loosed the chains of death around his Son because Jesus was perfectly holy and spotlessly righteous. It wasn't possible for the sinless King to be held by death.

Quoting Psalm 16:8–11, Peter makes the staggering claim that David himself, the premier king in Israel's history, anticipated the resurrection of Christ. In the psalm, David expressed his hope that God wouldn't abandon him to death, but Peter points out that this hope is realized only in Jesus. David's prayers pointed past himself to the eternal heir God promised would inherit his throne forever. And though King David died, and the pilgrims in Jerusalem could even stop by his tomb, King Jesus overcame the corruption of death in the fullest sense imaginable. Jesus was the true Holy One, raised from death, who answers David's prayer and shares his indestructible life with all who believe.

This Jesus, Peter testifies, was exalted in his ascension to the right hand of God the Father—the symbolic place of absolute power and authority—and he sent the promised Holy Spirit, whose work the Jewish audience has now seen and heard with their own eyes and ears. So what do the events of Pentecost mean? Peter has used the Scriptures they believe to interpret the phenomena they've seen. And with the Old Testament as his interpretive lens, Peter asserts that the happenings at Pentecost mean that Jesus has indeed been raised from the dead and has poured out his Spirit to fill God's new covenant people, all in accordance with the Scriptures. So the apostle confidently concludes, "Let all the house of Israel therefore know for certain that God has made him both Lord and Christ, this Jesus whom you crucified."[5]

Through Peter's preaching, the Holy Spirit performs his life giving work and cuts the people to the heart. If what Peter declares is really true, what must they do? They have to repent—agreeing with God about the sinfulness of their sin and looking in faith to Jesus—and enter the church through the covenant sign and seal of baptism. As rebels repent and are baptized in faith, they enter God's new covenant community and receive all the blessings God promised, including forgiveness and the gift of the indwelling Spirit. And this holds true not only for the Jews listening to Peter,

---

5. Acts 2:36.

but for every person—whether their children or those far away—whom the Lord sovereignly calls to himself.

In one day, the church grows from one hundred twenty to three thousand, dramatically confirming that the Spirit of God is with his people and that he's going to take the gospel to the ends of the earth through the proclamation and life of Christ's disciples. And while the Spirit's descent at Pentecost is a unique event in the history of salvation, the same Spirit who fell at Jerusalem still resides within all of God's people, and the same promises Peter announced that day are still the hope of every sinner that the Spirit has brought to faith in Christ. In the Old Testament, the feast of Pentecost celebrated God's faithfulness in giving the harvest, and the sending of the Spirit at Pentecost means the harvest of disciples is only beginning.

*Great God, thank you for keeping the promise you made so long ago to send your Holy Spirit to dwell within all your people. Give us eyes to see how your Scriptures find their ultimate meaning in the life, death, and resurrection of Jesus, and empower us by your Spirit to proclaim the good news of Christ to all who are far off, that they might join us as blessed children in your family of grace.*

# 34

# Righteous by Faith

*Romans 3:9—4:25*

WITH THIS MEDITATION, WE turn our attention to a new portion of Scripture. Up to this point in the New Testament, we've followed the historical narratives of the Gospels and Acts as they recounted the life of Jesus and the birth of the church. The climactic events of redemptive history have been accomplished through Jesus' life, death, resurrection, and ascension, and now the second coming of Christ is the only thing standing between the church and the completion of God's story. The New Testament epistles—the letters of Romans through Jude—don't advance the story of the word. They reflect on the story so that Christians will know how to faithfully play their part in God's drama. These epistles are given to nourish, strengthen, and direct the church as we trust Christ, speak the gospel, live as members of the kingdom, and anticipate the Lord's return.

The early chapters of Paul's epistle to the Romans make the case that the whole world—Jew and Gentile alike—stands equally guilty and condemned under the curse of sin. As evidence, Paul lists a number of Old Testament texts, most coming from the Psalms, that describe every human's fallen condition. The alienation and spiritual death that entered creation through Adam's rebellion in Eden have spread to all without exception, and this death is so pervasive that no person seeks after God or does what is righteous in his eyes, "not even one."[1] Left to our own devices, our hearts are so turned in on themselves that even our good deeds are bad, stained with selfishness and idolatry. And if this is our desperate condition, then

---

1. Rom 3:12, citing Ps 14:3.

## Part Three: From Christ's Ascension to Christ's Return

there's no hope of earning our approval and acceptance with God through our obedience, "for by works of the law no human being will be justified in his sight."[2] God's law can expose our sin, but it can't cure it.

*But.* This is one of the most precious words in the Bible. Once we've been brought low to recognize our utter inability to restore ourselves to God, the gospel raises us with the promise of God's saving grace: "But now the righteousness of God has been manifested apart from the law."[3] God demonstrates his promise keeping righteousness by giving us the righteousness we need in order to dwell in his presence. He counts us as having lived in perfect holiness *by faith in his Son*, without any reference to our personal obedience or merits.

And while this righteousness comes to us apart from the law, Paul agrees with Jesus that both the Law and the Prophets—in other words, the entire Old Testament—point to the sacrificial work of Christ as the way God will redeem his people. The whole point of the Bible's story has been that God alone can and will provide redemption. By offering up his Son as a propitiation that satisfies his wrath against sin, God gloriously proves himself to be both just and justifier. At the cross where Jesus took the death rebels deserve, God simultaneously punishes sin with perfect justice and graciously secures justification for sinners. With this kind of gospel, where the triune God does everything and sinners contribute nothing, there's no room for any kind of boasting or self-exaltation. There's only one worthy of praise.

In Romans 4, Paul uses Abraham as a case study to prove that justification has always been by God's grace through faith in his promises. Citing Genesis 15:6, Paul notes that "Abraham believed God, and it was counted to him as righteousness."[4] And Paul points out that David calls blessed "those whose lawless deeds are forgiven, and whose sins are covered."[5] So both the premier patriarch and the premier king in Israel's history direct our hope to a righteousness that's granted apart from our works, solely through faith in the God who justifies the ungodly.

But here Paul anticipates a question: Is the blessing of justification by faith in Christ only for the circumcised (the physical descendants of Abraham), or is it for Gentiles, too? To provide an answer, Paul takes us to the

2. Rom 3:20.
3. Rom 3:21.
4. Rom 4:3.
5. Rom 4:7, citing Ps 32:1.

details of Abraham's life. Abraham was counted righteous by faith before he ever received the sign and seal of circumcision. Paul argues that God intentionally did this to show that the righteousness that comes through faith isn't just for circumcised Jews, but for everyone who follows in the faith of Abraham, regardless of their family lineage. Just as Jew and Gentile are together condemned in sin, so they're together justified by faith in Christ. God promised Abraham a great family made up of a multitude of nations, and by faith in Jesus the nations are grafted into Abraham's spiritual family.

To those Jews still tempted to believe that their possession of the law gives them an advantage, Paul offers a reality check. If God's promises could be attained through obedience, then faith would be meaningless because salvation would ultimately depend on you and not on God, and the promise would be void because no spiritually dead human being could ever keep the law anyway. In fact, the Jews' possession of the law, far from giving them a head start on the road to self-salvation, actually brings a deeper level of accountability. Gentiles who don't have the law are still guilty of sin, but they aren't able to transgress the law in the same way by intentionally violating its revealed command. But Jews who do have the law are guilty of rejecting the revealed will of God in Scripture, and their greater knowledge of God brings a greater degree of judgment for their rebellion.

Don't miss the irony here: the very law some believe will get them to God actually magnifies the seriousness of their failures and intensifies their impending judgment. What's Paul's point? His point is that you can't use the law as your stepping stone to God because that was never its purpose. If you do, you'll miss the ways the law pushes you in repentance to Christ, and the law will only work for your condemnation.

Works based salvation is futile, a fool's deadly errand, but God's righteousness is granted through faith so that God might be exalted as the gracious giver of life and so that his promise might be guaranteed to every person who trusts the gospel. Abraham clung in faith to the covenant promises that pointed forward to Jesus, and his faith was "counted to him as righteousness."[6] And Paul says that those words were written for our sake so that we'd know that all who cling in faith to the covenant promises fulfilled in Jesus are justified by God's grace as well. Jesus died to take our death, and he was raised in righteousness so that we might be declared righteous in him.

So lay down the weary works you're using to earn your standing with God and rest by faith in the Christ who's done it all.

---

6. Rom 4:22, citing Gen 15:6.

## Part Three: From Christ's Ascension to Christ's Return

*Holy Father, on our own we're desperate creatures—spiritually dead and incapable of even seeking after you. If salvation depended on our obedience, we'd all be lost. But in your merciful kindness, you sent Jesus to the cross to magnify your glory as both the just judge of sin and the gracious justifier of ungodly sinners. We praise you for your faithfulness. We exalt you for your grace. And we ask that your Holy Spirit would fix our hope on Christ so that we might rest from our self-justifying efforts and enjoy the gifts of fellowship and acceptance that he died and rose again to purchase.*

# 35

# More Than Conquerors
## *Romans 8*

THIS PASSAGE HAS BEEN called by many the most beautiful chapter in the most beautiful letter in the most beautiful book ever penned. Romans 8 is a catalogue of the blessed assurances that belong to every child of the Father, every heir with Christ, every recipient of the Holy Spirit. Though life is often hard—though sin and suffering and opposition and death remain part of the Christian life—the gospel promises that God is with us and God is for us, and that hope that can sustain our faith, empower our joy, comfort our hearts, and animate our worship.

Ever since Adam's rebellion in the garden, humanity has lived under the power and penalty of sin and death. This is what Paul has in mind when he says that sinners are "in the flesh." Our dead hearts are slaves to false gods—unable to submit to God's law or please him. Our idolatry has invited God's just condemnation and wrath. And our love affair with sin thrusts us into a living death that will eventually lead to eternal death. Apart from divine intervention, our whole lives are "in the flesh"—defined by opposition to God.

But for the one who is in the Spirit—who has been made new, united to Christ, and indwelt by the Holy Spirit—"there is now therefore no condemnation."[1] Jesus took on humanity through his incarnation, obeyed God completely in his life, and bore the sentence for sin in his crucifixion in order to perfectly fulfill all of the law's demands for us. No condemnation remains for the believer because Jesus took our condemnation in full.

1. Rom 8:1.

## Part Three: From Christ's Ascension to Christ's Return

When accusations abound and your heart is tempted to believe that a holy God would have no part of you, this precious promise that you're righteous and acceptable because of Christ's work is one you must return to again and again.

The penalty is gone, but those in the Spirit are also liberated from the *power* of sin and death. The Spirit grants his people new hearts that are able to trust, love, and submit to God as we hope in the gospel. No longer do we have to walk in living death, controlled by idolatrous desires that never truly satisfy. Instead, we can and must walk in the Spirit—in fellowship with God, embodying the identity we've been given by grace, looking to his provision and promises in Christ to meet all of our needs in a way that radiates outward in joyful obedience. And this spiritual life that we enjoy now will never end. Paul ensures us that the Father who raised his Son from the dead will "give life to your mortal bodies"[2] through the very Spirit who presently dwells within us. In Christ and by his Spirit, God is undoing all the devastation that was wrought by the fall.

Paul continues by confirming that everyone who possesses the Spirit is a son of God. The true Son left his home with the Father and went to the cross so that we who had run from the Father could be welcomed as sons. And make no mistake, this blessing of sonship is for men and women alike. In first-century Rome, only sons were permitted to inherit, but in Christ, every sinner is made a son and heir to all the riches of grace that the Father bestows upon his children. And the Holy Spirit who empowers our pleas to our Father also testifies to our hearts that we're sons of God, ministering to us God's gospel word so that we can rest in his fatherly love.

We might be tempted to believe that, because we are God's children, life will therefore be a breeze. But Paul reminds us that if Jesus suffered before entering glory, then everyone who's an heir with him by faith must also walk in the way of the cross, suffering with Christ before being glorified with him. Not only is hardship inevitable in a broken world. For the Christian, suffering is a mark of sonship and part of the God-ordained path to glory.

Lest you despair at the difficulties you're experiencing now or that lie ahead, Paul assures you that "the sufferings of this present time are not worth comparing with the glory that is to be revealed to us."[3] We may find this profoundly difficult to believe, but Paul—who suffered mightily in his

2. Rom 8:11.
3. Rom 8:18.

own right—is utterly convinced that the restoration, healing, and joy that lie ahead for God's children are so wondrous and complete that this future hope can sustain our faith in the face of any trial. The entire universe, thrust into futility by humanity's rebellion, will be renewed and set free from its corruption, and we who belong to God by faith will live eternally in the holy presence of our Father with resurrected bodies that will never again feel the sting of decay and death.

Nevertheless, our suffering is often clouded with confusion because, as finite creatures, we can't know precisely what God is doing in all the details of our pain. But for these moments, Paul offers two comforts. First, when our ignorance of God's secret purposes leaves us unsure about how to specifically pray in hard circumstances, the Holy Spirit himself—who always prays in line with God's will—intercedes for us. Second, those who love God and are called according to his purpose can know that everything God ordains, he ordains for their good. How can Paul be so sure? Because every person whom God foreknew and set his gracious affection upon, he predestined to be conformed to the image of Christ. And everyone he predestined, he in turn calls to faith, justifies, and will one day glorify. From eternity past, God has been committed to the total salvation of the people he chose for himself by grace, and that means that he's sovereignly using every aspect of believers' lives to grow us in faith and holiness and eventually bring us into his restored kingdom—and that is most certainly for our good.

Paul concludes chapter 8, and this entire section of the book of Romans, with a celebration of the confidence and security that believers have because of Christ's work. Though physical and spiritual enemies attack, no opposition can prevail over those who have God as their refuge and defender. Though circumstances may give the impression that God has forgotten us, we can rejoice that the Father who gave his only Son for us will certainly provide everything we could ever need for life and faithfulness. Though charges are hurled at us—sometimes from our very own hearts—Jesus died for our sin, rose in righteous victory, and now intercedes for us at the right hand of God.

And since God demonstrated his love for his people and brought us into fellowship with himself in the cross of Christ, nothing in all of creation—not even your sin—can drive a wedge between you and God's gracious, steadfast covenant love. In fact, God makes us "more than

## Part Three: From Christ's Ascension to Christ's Return

conquerors"[4] over our tribulations. He not only brings us through them by grace. He takes what would threaten to destroy us and uses it powerfully and lovingly for our good, to refine our faith and grow us in holiness.

May these precious gospel assurances fill you with joy and empower your perseverance.

*Blessed God, we rejoice that there is now no condemnation from the Father for anyone who is united to Christ by faith and indwelt by your Holy Spirit. No longer in the flesh, help us to walk as those who are in the Spirit—living by faith as children who've been graciously restored to fellowship with you. Comfort our weary hearts with the unshakable promises of your gospel so that we might rest in your love and stand firm in the faith.*

---

4. Rom 8:37.

# 36

# Living Sacrifices

## *Romans 12*

HAVING EXPLORED OUR NEED for the gospel, the content of the gospel, and the various blessings of the gospel, Paul turns his attention in Romans 12 to the conduct—the comprehensive response of faith, worship, and obedience—that the gospel empowers. The cross brings reconciliation and restoration where sin brought alienation and destruction, so Paul exhorts Christians to live in the fellowship with God and one another that we've been granted in Christ and by the Spirit.

In the New Testament, the scriptural commands to believers are always grounded in the accomplishments of Christ. That's why Paul begins verse 1 this way: "I appeal to you *therefore*, brothers, *by the mercies of God*."[1] Paul spent the first eleven chapters of Romans laying a foundation of gospel grace. Only then does he shift his focus to the life of covenant faithfulness made possible and motivated by all the mercies of God. What Christians are to do in our lives always flows out of what Jesus did in his.

In light of God's salvation-securing work in the gospel, the only appropriate response for believers is to offer our whole selves as living sacrifices. The elaborate system of sacrifices outlined in the Old Testament clarified humanity's need for forgiveness and pointed forward to the once and for all sacrifice of Christ, and the offering of our Passover lamb has now made such sacrifices obsolete. But the sacrificial system continues in a different way. In Christ, believers are made priests who continually offer the spiritual sacrifices of worship and obedience to God. These are no longer the

---

1. Rom 12:1, emphasis added.

PART THREE: FROM CHRIST'S ASCENSION TO CHRIST'S RETURN

dead animals of old covenant ritual, but the living sacrifices of our entire existence, completely devoted to God. Jesus' sacrifice of atonement settled our standing with God so that our lives could be sacrifices of thanksgiving, offered in holiness for the pleasure of the Father.

This life of consecration, worship, and thanksgiving can only emerge as we're transformed by God's gracious truth—renewed in our affections, our beliefs, and our vision of the world. When we were dead in sin, we followed after the world in its rebellion against God and pursuit of idols. Our whole way of thinking, living, and loving was shaped by the narratives and priorities of a world in hostility toward God. Now that we're alive to God in Christ, his story has to permeate every part of who we are, reshaping our desires, our worldview, our moral compass, and our character. As God's word—centered on the person and work of Christ—re-narrates our lives, we grow in our ability not only to understand but also to delight in and obey God's revealed will for his creation.

With verse 3, Paul delves into what this gospel-transformed life specifically looks like, and he begins with humility. In our personal estimations of ourselves, we're to use sober judgment that lines up with the measure (or standard) of faith God has assigned. What does that mean? It doesn't mean that we consider ourselves based upon *how much* faith we have. Rather, it's a call to consider ourselves based on *the* faith handed to us in the message of the gospel. The cross tells us that our condition in sin was so desperate that only the death of God's Son could purchase our salvation. When we measure ourselves according to that message, the root of pride begins to wither and die. And this gospel driven humility will seep into our relationships as well, fueling our joyful service to the other members of Christ's body. Empowered by the good news that Jesus gladly served us at infinite personal cost, Christians can minister to one another—even, and especially, when it's costly—with every opportunity that the Spirit graciously provides.

The second fundamental Christian characteristic that Paul commends to us is love. "Let love be genuine"[2] stands as a summary of verses 9–21, but the sincere love that the gospel creates in us is a multi-faceted love that bursts outward in different directions.

First, believers must walk in genuine love *toward God*. God initiated a covenant relationship with us, setting his love on us before the foundation of the world and sending his only Son to bring us to himself as his special possession. Having received such an abundant love from God, Christians

2. Rom 12:9.

have every reason to offer our love to God in return. We don't love in order to be loved. We love because we have been and are loved. And this Godward love will cause us to hate what God hates, approve of what God approves, serve him with zeal, rejoice in the hope of the gospel, patiently trust the Lord through trials, and run to him in constant prayer.

Second, believers must walk in love *toward one another*. Jesus lived, died, and rose again to guarantee our adoption into God's family, together with every other Christian who calls on his name. Paul urges us to love one another with brotherly affection because that's precisely what we are. God has made us brothers in Christ. When we regularly recognize that our elder brother Jesus gave himself to bind us as family to our fellow believers, we'll begin to count it a joy to honor, care for, welcome, weep with, celebrate with, and associate with one another—in spite of the sin that continues to dwell within our community.

Finally, believers must walk in love *toward our enemies*. Echoing the teachings of Jesus himself, Paul urges us to love the enemies who seek our harm by returning cursing with blessing and seeking to live at peace with everyone whom the Lord brings into our lives. Earlier, Paul noted that "while we were still sinners, Christ died for us,"[3] and this offers a powerful motive for enemy love.

But that's not the motive he offers here. Instead, he cites an Old Testament promise of judgment: "Vengeance is mine, I will repay, says the Lord."[4] We might initially assume that God's vengeance serves to promote our vengeance, but Paul asserts that exactly the opposite is true. God's vengeance makes possible our peace. God promises to judge all sin with perfect wisdom and justice—either through the cross of Christ at Golgotha or the judgment of Christ at the end of the age. If you believe that final justice is up to you to administer, you'll either become an oppressor yourself, or you'll give up on the possibility of justice altogether. But when you trust that God will ultimately take care of justice, you can seek to overcome evil with good in a way that stirs repentance in your enemies and commends the gospel to all through your honorable living.

So God empowers transformed lives by his grace, and he graciously uses transformed lives to bring others to faith in and knowledge of his Son.

---

3. Rom 5:8.
4. Rom 12:19, citing Deut 32:35.

## Part Three: From Christ's Ascension to Christ's Return

*Merciful God, we praise you for bringing us into your covenant family through the gracious work of Jesus. In light of your gospel mercies, help us to offer our whole selves as living sacrifices as you renew our minds with the Christ-centered story of your word. Humble us in the shadow of the cross that we might walk in humility. Fuel our love with the promise that you loved us first. And empower our mercy as we rest in your complete and perfect justice.*

# 37

# The Foolishness of God

## 1 Corinthians 1:10—2:5

It's very easy for us—two millennia into this new covenant chapter of God's story—to romanticize life in the early church. Surely those young communities must have been perfect pictures of righteousness and love. After all, many of them were planted and visited by the apostles! But the New Testament won't permit this illusion. In fact, many of the epistles were written to confront specific problems in faith and practice that were springing up within the local churches of the first century. The first generations of Christians dealt with all the temptations we deal with today, but the consistent testimony of Scripture is that the gospel is sufficient to cover our continuing failures and empower progress in holiness so that the church might more fully reflect the character and beauty of her Lord and his kingdom.

In Paul's first letter to the church at Corinth, the blemishes of God's people and the transforming grace of the gospel are both on full display. News had reached Paul that divisions were cropping up in the church as groups began identifying themselves with particular leaders. Arguments were breaking out within the church as each faction arrogantly sought to persuade the others that their leader—and hence their camp—was the wisest and most spiritually advanced.

Paul responds with a litany of rhetorical questions in verse 13. *Is Christ divided?* No, Jesus purchased one body for himself over which he is head and Lord. *Was Paul crucified for you?* Of course not, and it's therefore completely inappropriate for Christians to hitch their ultimate identity or offer their fundamental allegiance to any leader other than Jesus himself. *Were you baptized in the name of Paul?* By no means, but believers are baptized

## Part Three: From Christ's Ascension to Christ's Return

into the name of the triune God and must accordingly walk as one in loving fellowship with every brother and sister who's received God's grace in Christ. Paul's questions are intended to wake the Corinthians up and force them to confront just how inconsistent their divisiveness is with what Jesus accomplished in his death and resurrection. In a world like ours—saturated with celebrity, where identification with one charismatic leader or another can so quickly lead toward spiritual pride—Paul's call for unity in devotion to Christ and love for one another is as necessary as ever.

Paul insightfully recognizes that the self-exaltation taking place in the Corinthian church isn't merely a relational problem. It's a theological problem that goes straight to the core of the gospel message. Pride can only thrive where there's a fundamental misunderstanding of God's work in Jesus. So he challenges their inflated egos with three beautiful truths that, if internalized, will promote a proper self-understanding and love for the body of Christ.

*First, the message of the cross is foolishness and weakness to the world.* Paul challenges the allegedly wise Corinthians by reminding them of the content of the gospel. The central message of Christianity is that the Son of God took on human flesh in order to die and rescue his enemies. Divinity taking on flesh? Power directed toward service rather than domination? The Son of God submitting to the horrors of the cross? According to the logic of a fallen world, this message is utter foolishness, but to those who've been given eyes to see and hearts to savor the glory of God in Christ, the gospel is the precious wisdom and power of God.

If God saw fit to redeem his people through the humiliating weakness of the cross, if the church is brought into existence through the apparent defeat of her God, if the banner over us reads "people of the crucified Lord," then it just doesn't make sense for Christians to waste their time in self-promotion in order to be seen as wise. When you see that Jesus' weakness is your greatest strength, you don't have to pretend to be strong anymore. Rather, clinging in hope to the foolishness of God that turns upside-down the wisdom of the world, the church can embrace meekness and lowliness as she follows after her cross-bearing King.

*Second, God chooses the foolish and the weak for his glory.* Paul basically encourages the Corinthians to take a good look in the mirror: "Not many of you were wise according to worldly standards, not many were powerful, not many were of noble birth."[1] Translation: you're not that impressive.

---

1. 1 Cor 1:26.

## The Foolishness of God

But God's gospel is all about restoring people who know that they're weak, broken, and lowly. Jesus taught that he, our great physician, came not for the well who wrongly believe they're wise, strong, and righteous apart from God. He came for the sick who recognize just how deeply they need his grace—and that's a message that the powerful of the world are often much slower to receive precisely because they have so much to lose by dying to themselves in repentance.

And what is God's purpose in choosing the weak by grace? "That no human being might boast in the presence of God."[2] In other words, if the only wisdom, righteousness, salvation, and status you can lay claim to is the wisdom, righteousness, salvation, and status granted to you by God in Jesus, then your arrogant boasting will fade away as you joyfully exalt the glory of the God who blessed you despite your unimpressive pedigree, simply because he delights in exercising grace. No Christian can simultaneously imagine that both he and Jesus are worthy of praise.

*Third, true gospel ministry matches the weakness of the gospel message.* The Corinthians were aligning themselves with prominent church leaders, but when Paul considers his own ministry, he notes how preposterous this sort of Christianized hero worship really is. Paul didn't dress his preaching with rhetorical flourishes or dazzling oratorical techniques. He didn't travel with a public relations team or market his ministry "brand." He embodied in his ministry the weakness of the Christ he preached. His reasoning? Showy, manipulative methods risk eclipsing the work of Christ with personality and winning people to merely human wisdom. But when the gospel is humbly articulated by someone who's willing to be eclipsed by the glories of God's grace, then any fruitfulness can be confidently credited to the Holy Spirit powerfully bringing sinners to repentance and faith in Jesus.

The very character of Paul's ministry reveals how wrong-headed the Corinthians' factionalism is. Why would they base their identity on any particular minister when true ministry allows self to recede to the background and points to the surpassing glories of Jesus? Even today, we still love the feeling of significance that comes from associating ourselves with prominent figures, and leaders love the feeling of significance that comes from being the focus of a massive following. This is a dangerous combination, and both the church and her ministers have to regularly consider how the gospel addresses these all-too-human temptations and draws both shepherds and sheep into the exclusive worship of Christ.

2. 1 Cor 1:29.

## Part Three: From Christ's Ascension to Christ's Return

How then can we walk in unity and put to death our prideful longing to be seen as wise? We have to know Jesus as the Lord who was willingly brought low to bring us to God. We have to know ourselves as sinful, broken beggars whose only boast is in the Lord. And we have to know that genuine, gospel-shaped ministry takes not only its message, but also its form, from the foolish and yet gloriously wise message of the cross.

*Great and gracious God, we confess that we're far too quick to fancy ourselves wise in ways that contradict the gospel of your Son. Help us delight in lowliness as we cling by faith to a Christ who was rejected by the world. Grow us in humility as we see the depths of our sin and the heights of your mercy. Break us of the idolatrous need to exalt ourselves that inevitably results in division, and as we look in hope to the Lord Jesus, bind us in love and fellowship with all your saints.*

# 38

# By Faith or by Works?
## *Galatians 3:1–14*

STARTLING NEWS HAS REACHED Paul concerning the church in Galatia. Infiltrated by false teachers, a church which formerly received the good news of Christ with faith is now flirting with a new "gospel." These teachers have convinced the Galatians that they have to adhere to the old covenant law—in essence, they have to become Jewish by submitting to circumcision and embracing all the regulations of the Mosaic code—in order to truly belong to God's people: "Sure, you need to trust Jesus, but you *also* need to adhere to the law. Jesus does his part, and you do yours."

But this new gospel is no gospel at all. Whenever the sufficiency of the cross is called into question, whenever our works are added to the atoning work of Christ, God's grace is voided and replaced by human merit.

Why is this kind of message so seductive? Because despite all the anxiety and insecurity it brings, we love believing that we're in control of our own destiny. We exult in the notion that our standing before God is ultimately in our hands. Our pride is fed and our egos intoxicated when we entertain the thought that our actions determine God's love for and acceptance of us.

And this isn't merely an ancient heresy. It's alive and well today. How many Christians live in perpetual fear, languish in insecurity, or dwell in bondage to pride because they've been led to believe that, while Jesus offers them forgiveness, it's now their duty to keep and increase God's love for them by their obedience? The false teaching that took root in Galatia lives on in our hearts whenever we seek to have a hand in securing any part of our salvation.

# Part Three: From Christ's Ascension to Christ's Return

"O foolish Galatians! Who has bewitched you?"[1] This language seems harsh, but Paul is driven by zealous love for Christ's church and therefore desires to snap the Galatians back from their dangerous, self-justifying slumber. In an effort to expose their foolishness, the apostle peppers them with questions. *Did you first receive the Spirit by faith in Christ's gospel or by your obedience to the law?* They received the gift of the Holy Spirit—together with all the other blessings of the new covenant—when they beheld the crucified Lord with the eyes of their hearts, hearing and believing the gospel of grace in Jesus. They began the Christian life by grace through faith. Their moral obedience and fitness had nothing to do with it.

*So if you began by the Spirit, trusting the Christ to whom the Spirit always points, are you now being brought to completion through your own efforts to keep the law?* By no means! Jesus didn't start something by grace that you have to finish by works. On the contrary, the very gospel that brings us into God's family is the gospel that keeps us in his fatherly affection and grows us more and more to look and live like the children of God we already are.

To say it another way, the gospel isn't simply a message for conversion. It's a message for the converted, too. The only way we can keep from reverting back to the self-saving methods of the flesh and striving to increase God's affection for us through our obedience is to believe and re-appropriate the gospel every day. We have to trust that Christ's life, death, and resurrection on our behalf is enough to ensure that God's love is still ours by grace.

And that's how true growth in holiness and Christ-likeness happens, too—by believing and re-appropriating the gospel every day. We don't make progress in the Christian life by moving on from the gospel, but by applying the gospel to all the different realms of life. In the cross, God has met our every need by giving us himself and all the blessings of fellowship with him. The grip that our idols hold on our hearts begins to weaken, and we can begin to walk in Godward obedience and worship, as we see ever more clearly that everything we've ever needed we've already been granted in the gospel. The people-pleaser who lives for the approval of others can live to please God only as she sees that God has already granted her the ultimate form of approval in the gospel of Christ. The penny-pincher who uses money as his source of security can grow in generosity only as he finds that his life is safe in covenant with God on the basis of Christ's death and

---

1. Gal 3:1.

resurrection. God initially saves us through faith in the gospel, and he continually shapes us by faith in the gospel, too.

The false teachers in Galatia proclaimed that, in order to be acceptable to God, you must not only believe in Christ but also live like an Israelite, keeping all of the old covenant laws. So Paul goes all the way back to Israel's beginnings in God's covenant with Abraham, and he shows that the father of the Jewish nation is proof that salvation is granted by faith and not by works. According to Genesis 15:6, Abraham was counted righteous—he was given a status of righteousness that he'd done nothing to deserve—simply because he trusted the gracious promises of God. That means that the true "son of Abraham," the true Israelite, the true member of God's covenant people, isn't the one who relies on obedience to the law, but who follows Abraham in trusting God's saving promises.

When we try to earn God's acceptance through obedience, we inevitably elevate the aspects of the law we find easy to keep and ignore the commands we consider difficult or unrealistic. Downplaying parts of God's law is really the only way we can cope with the pressure to perform. But Paul reminds us, "Cursed be everyone who does not abide by *all things* written in the Book of the Law, and do them."[2] If you depend on your moral goodness to secure your blessing from God, you'll find only a curse, and that's because the law demands a complete obedience from the heart that no fallen human being can muster.

But in Christ, God offers us by grace the blessing which we could never merit by our works. How? Paul already mentioned that the Lord preached the gospel in shadow form to Abraham when he vowed that the nations would be blessed through his family. And that shadow gave way to substance when Jesus—Abraham's faithful descendant—went to the cross so that Jew and Gentile alike might experience the blessings of life in God's kingdom by faith. In the Old Testament, hanging someone on a tree served as a sign that a person was under God's curse, so when Jesus was hanged on his tree, it was a public declaration that he was bearing God's curse against sin. Jesus took the curse we deserved so that we might receive the blessing he deserved, and the only way to receive that blessing is to stop striving for acceptance and hope in the Christ whose death is your covering and whose life is your righteousness.

The gospel you trusted when you became a Christian is the gospel you have to trust for the entirety of the Christian life, because the gospel that

---

2. Gal 3:10, citing Deut 27:26, emphasis added.

## Part Three: From Christ's Ascension to Christ's Return

brought you into God's family is the gospel that keeps you there and grows you to resemble the Father who made you his child.

*Lord, how easily we move from trusting Christ's work in the gospel to relying on our works—whether to earn your love, keep your love, increase your love, or grow us into maturity. Open our eyes to see that the pursuit of blessing through the law only leaves us under the curse of sin that our disobedience deserves. Turn our hearts in faith to the Christ who bore the curse on our behalf so that we could receive all the blessings of fellowship with you. And grow us in the worship and obedience that glorifies your name as we plumb the depths of the gospel and find that in Christ you've given us everything we could ever desire.*

# 39

# Walk by the Spirit

*Galatians 5:16—6:10*

EVERY CHRISTIAN HAS BEEN made spiritually alive by the Holy Spirit, given a new heart that worships God and clings to the gracious gospel of Christ's life, death, and resurrection. And yet within each of us, a war rages on: "For the desires of the flesh are against the Spirit, and the desires of the Spirit are against the flesh, for these are opposed to each other, to keep you from doing the things you want to do."[1] The new birth is the beginning of a transformation that will ultimately reach its completion when every child of God is raised and glorified with the Lord Jesus. But in the meantime, believers must live with the painful reality that we possess divided hearts which, while alive to God, still often teem with desires that lead us to trust and serve idols for our meaning, satisfaction, wholeness, and justification.

So Paul exhorts us to prepare for the battle: "But I say, walk by the Spirit, and you will not gratify the desires of the flesh."[2] But what does this mean? Christians frequently speak of yielding, following, and submitting to the Holy Spirit, but this can be left so abstract that it's completely unhelpful. "Walking by the Spirit" is Paul's shorthand way of encouraging believers to constantly hope and live in light of the finished work of Christ in the gospel. Jesus promised his disciples that the Holy Spirit would bear witness about and glorify him,[3] so to walk by the Spirit is to consistently look in faith to the Christ to whom the Spirit points us. It's to walk in our new identity by

1. Gal 5:17.
2. Gal 5:16.
3. See John 15:26; 16:14.

faith, to regularly re-appropriate the truths of the gospel to our hearts such that we live as if all the blessings of grace are truly ours in Jesus.

This is how believers fight against the desires of our sinful hearts. Our old selves naturally and deceptively turn good things into gods by looking to them for a form of salvation and life. Control, acceptance, power, comfort, money, relationships, family, and all sorts of other created things get exalted to the status of non-negotiable must-haves—our functional saviors—so our hearts worship them, and our lives become devoted to gaining, keeping, and serving them in ways that dishonor God and leave us in bondage.

But as we apply the truths of the gospel to our hearts, we find that we no longer have to search for life in our idols. We're finally free. You don't have to find your security in controlling every detail of your life when you know that the God who gave his Son for you is in control. You don't have to chase temporary comforts when God has offered you the ultimate comfort in reconciliation with him through Christ. You don't have to use money or power or relationships as a way to attain a sense of approval when the gospel tells you God's pleasure is eternally yours because of the cross. Walking in the Spirit by returning again and again to the gospel chips away at the idolatrous desires of the flesh and enables us to walk in God-exalting holiness as we see that all of our deepest needs have been met in Jesus.

As we walk by the Spirit, the gospel empowers us to obey God's will. But Paul would remind us, "If you are led by the Spirit, you are not under the law."[4] There's a paradox here. If you put yourself under the law—trying to earn your status with God through your obedience—you'll never be able to actually obey the law because all your works will be tainted by your narcissistic pursuit of self-salvation. You'll be obeying for you and your glory, not for God and his, and that kind of obedience is ultimately disobedience. But if you know that Jesus fulfilled the law for you and reconciled you to God, you can obey God from a heart of worship and thanksgiving that rests secure in his grace.

Paul offers contrasting pictures of what life looks like when we're walking in the flesh and in the Spirit. Idolatry breeds sexual sin as we use our bodies and the bodies of others to achieve a sense of fulfillment, healing, and significance. It leads to faulty religion as we construct gods that can be manipulated to give us what we want. It leads to relational disharmony as we begin to see people not as people but as a means to our idolatrous ends.

4. Gal 5:18.

And it leads to misuses of God's good creation as we seek the salvation only God can provide in the gifts rather than the Giver. Paul warns us: those whose lives are characterized by the persistent and unrepentant works of the flesh don't belong to God by faith and therefore won't inherit his kingdom. Indeed, one of the distinguishing marks of the Christian is that he has crucified the flesh—she's taken her idols to the cross in repentance and regularly seeks to put them to death in the power of the gospel.

When we walk in the Spirit by trusting Christ, the works of the flesh are replaced by the fruit of the Spirit. The Spirit grows us up into faithful obedience and maturity as he feeds our hearts with the nourishing grace of the gospel. It's important to note two things about Paul's list.

*First, idolatry can manufacture a fake form of fruit that can be quite difficult to recognize.* False love selfishly loves people for what you get out of them, but genuine love graciously seeks their good apart from what they can do for you and is extended even to the people you don't find easily lovable. False joy is grounded in having life go how you want, but genuine joy is fueled by God's character and promises and therefore can persevere even in the valley. Imposter fruit grows in the soil of idolatry, but true fruit only springs from the soil of a heart that's regularly watered with the gospel.

*Second, Paul refers to a single fruit.* Each trait is but one dimension of a gospel-shaped character. If you find it easy to be kind in service to others but rarely experience peace, it may be that your kindness is simply an attempt to gain people's love that leaves you insecure and anxious. If you're a master of self-control but fail to exercise gentleness in your relationships with others, your self-control may just be a prideful way to prove your righteousness that results in harsh evaluations of others. But when you walk in the Spirit, applying all the benefits of the gospel to all the dark corners of your heart, you'll be able to walk in both kindness *and* peace, self-control *and* gentleness. The different aspects of the fruit of the Spirit will grow together.

No doubt because the relationships in the Galatian church were a wreck, Paul puts special emphasis on how walking in the Spirit fosters peace with others. Whenever we try to secure our salvation through an idol, we become conceited and self-absorbed in one of two ways: either we look down on people in pride and provoke them because they don't measure up to us, or we gaze upward at them in envy and malice because we don't measure up to them.

# Part Three: From Christ's Ascension to Christ's Return

The gospel, however, enables us to take our eyes off ourselves by telling us our identity depends on Jesus, not us. Pride is destroyed by the humbling truth that we're sinners saved by grace, and envy is destroyed by the emboldening truth that we already possess more than we could ask or imagine in Christ. This makes it possible for us to lovingly confront a straying brother with both courage and humility, bearing their burdens with them in solidarity and love. And rather than constantly comparing ourselves to others, we'll be able to evaluate ourselves honestly in light of God's law, knowing that our acceptance with him has already been secured.

Paul ends by urging believers to persevere in the Spirit. There are times in this age between Jesus' first and second comings when it seems that sin—with all of its indulgence—leads to the life of pleasure, fulfillment, and blessing. But don't be duped: "God is not mocked, for whatever one sows, that will he also reap."[5] If your existence is spent consistently and unrepentantly sowing to the flesh, though you may enjoy the fleeting thrills of idolatry, you'll reap death both now and forever. Your life will begin to unravel as every part of you is affected by your slavery to idols, and this living death will extend into eternity as you bear the holy judgment of God.

But if you sow to the Spirit in repentance and faith, you'll experience a taste of the *shalom* of fellowship with God now which you'll experience in full in the presence of the triune God in his never-ending kingdom. Walking in the Spirit, then, is the way of true life and joy.

*Gracious God, as your Spirit ever points us to the finished work of Christ and all the blessings he secured, help us to walk in the Spirit—applying your gospel to our whole lives—that we might put to death our idolatrous desires and deeds, bearing the fruit of faith and obedience to the glory of your name.*

---

5. Gal 6:7.

# 40

# The Riches of Grace

## *Ephesians 1:3—2:22*

WE'VE SEEN GOD'S GRACE—HIS completely free and undeserved favor—in action throughout the story of the word. By grace, God issued a promise to Adam and Eve when their sin had merited only condemnation and death. By grace, he delivered Noah and his family through the flood of his judgment. By grace, he entered into a covenant with Abraham to bring restoration and healing to the nations. By grace, he persevered in faithfulness to Israel despite her frequent disobedience and rebellion. And by grace, he sent his Son into the world to live, die, and rise again and free his people from the power and penalty of sin. We've seen God's grace permeating redemptive history, but in the book of Ephesians, Paul offers us what may be the fullest and most comprehensive exposition of God's grace in the whole Bible. And the riches of this grace press us low in humility and lift us high in joyful worship at the exact same time.

    Paul begins with a doxology, an expression of praise to the Lord, that simultaneously blesses God while reminding us of the depths of the Trinitarian grace that extends from eternity past to eternity future. The Father, before the foundation of the world, sovereignly chose those upon whom he set his free, redeeming love and purposed to bring them into fellowship with himself. In his wisdom and mercy, "he predestined us for adoption as sons through Jesus Christ,"[1] the Son who offered himself at the cross to accomplish our redemption, the Son who shares all the blessings of his life and death with every sinner united to him by faith. And God grants us his

---

1. Eph 1:5.

## Part Three: From Christ's Ascension to Christ's Return

Holy Spirit as a seal who marks us as irrevocably belonging to God and as a down payment—a first installment of a tremendous treasure—who points to and guarantees the full inheritance of life with God that awaits us in the new heavens and new earth.

Why would God do this? Why would the self-sufficient, supremely joyful triune God determine before time to love wicked creatures who don't deserve his love, to die in place of their death, to shower them with the riches of union and communion with him, and to indwell them until he graciously brings them into his eternal kingdom? The ultimate purpose underneath all of God's workings in history is to reveal the multifaceted, soul-satisfying glory of his name. He works "to the praise of his glory"[2] so that the brilliance and worth of his character radiates through his universe and is magnified in the worshiping hearts of his people.

Paul transitions from praising God for his grace to praying that Christians who've received such grace will grow to understand, treasure, and live in light of it. He begs the Spirit to do what he's promised to do: to point his people to the finished work of Jesus and enlighten the eyes of our hearts so that we see, cling to, and delight in his glorious provision. And this Spirit-given knowledge of God reshapes how the church lives as God's kingdom people. The hope of forgiveness, adoption, and eternal life that Jesus purchased at the cross will empower your stability, peace, and abiding joy. The inheritance you've received in Jesus—an inheritance that literally consists of God himself—will make possible a profound contentment and deep thanksgiving throughout your life. And the conquering power over sin, death, and Satan demonstrated in Christ's resurrection and ascension will result in humble confidence that nothing can stand in the way of what God has promised to do in you, in his church, and in the world. Yet again, we see the New Testament's emphasis not on moving on from the gospel, but on growing with and by the gospel.

With the beginning of chapter 2, Paul reminds the Ephesians of how they (and every Christian with them) came to experience the grace of God. We were dead in our sin, following after the world, the flesh, and the devil—slaves to our idolatrous desires and under God's holy wrath. If Paul had said we were merely sick, there'd be some hope that we could contribute to our recovery. But lifeless people can't make themselves alive. Someone has to come from the outside to grant life to the dead.

---

2. Eph 1:14; cf. vv. 6, 12.

## The Riches of Grace

"But God . . . made us alive together with Christ."[3] This is the one-sided nature of grace. God gave us new hearts and united us to Jesus so that we now share in his resurrection life and are "seated with him in the heavenly places."[4] You have access to God's presence, a home in God's kingdom, and a share in all the blessings Jesus deserves as the truly righteous royal Son. We may be tempted to believe that we at least contributed our faith to the equation, but Paul declares that this faith too is a gift of God's grace. And if we can't even take credit for the faith that grabs hold of the cross, that means no one can boast about their salvation. God alone is responsible for your redemption, and God alone is worthy of glory. *But at least my good works are my own doing!* No, God prepared those beforehand that you might walk in them as he forms you in Christ for holiness by the hope of his gospel. The whole Christian life, through and through, from beginning to end, is all of grace,

Having traced God's grace in the Ephesians' transition from death to life, Paul urges them to remember that there was a time when Gentiles like them were separated from God's covenant people and were therefore strangers to his promises. God gave his covenant to Abraham's family, and under the old covenant, Gentiles who believed God's promises had to enter into Israel and come under the Mosaic law—with all of its distinguishing rituals. But in his life, death, and resurrection, Jesus fulfilled everything the Mosaic code anticipated, so belonging to the covenant people no longer requires entering into Israel, but entering into Jesus. Both Jew and Gentile become members of God's new covenant community—citizens of the true Israel—by faith in Christ's cross.

The new covenant erases the dividing line between ethnic Jews and ethnic Gentiles by reconciling all kinds of people to God through the gospel. Every member of Jesus' church has access in one Spirit through one Christ to one Father, restored in fellowship to God and therefore to one another. This means that, regardless of race or ethnicity or sex or cultural heritage, everyone who trusts the gospel is a citizen in God's kingdom, a child in God's household, and a living stone in the temple where God's presence dwells. There is no greater power for counter-cultural unity—the kind of unity that defies the expectations and conventions of the world—than the gospel of God's grace.

---

3. Eph 2:4–5.
4. Eph 2:6.

## Part Three: From Christ's Ascension to Christ's Return

*Gracious God, as we recall all the blessings of your undeserved kindness toward us in Jesus, we bless your name. Grow us in the knowledge of your grace. Fill our hearts with thanksgiving. Cultivate in us humility. And help us to walk in loving unity as one body restored to one God through one gospel.*

# 41

# To Live Is Christ, To Die Is Gain
## *Philippians 1:18b–2:11*

JESUS PROMISED HIS CHURCH that the life of faith between his first and second comings would be painful, that the road his people walk would be full of hardship and opposition from a world in rebellion against God. Like many of the apostles, Paul experienced such suffering firsthand, and he wrote his letter to the Philippian church while in prison for preaching the gospel. But while it might be natural to see his incarceration as a defeat—as cause for despair—Paul instead assures them that "what has happened to me has really served to advance the gospel"[1] and finds himself uniquely able to apply the gospel to the Philippians and to us so that we might persevere in faithfulness in the face of oppression and suffering.

Opposition for the sake of the gospel is never easy, whether it takes the form of imprisonment and execution or cultural marginalization and broken relationships. And yet Paul—and every Christian who shares his hope in Christ—has reason to rejoice in the hardship. Why? Paul can rejoice because he knows that he'll ultimately be delivered, not necessarily through his release from prison, but most assuredly through his resurrection and eternal life in the presence of God. He can rejoice because he knows that whatever shame he's received from his accusers will be overturned when God vindicates his faithful children on the last day. And he can rejoice because he knows that Jesus will be glorified both in his life and in his death as he clings in hope to the gospel.

---

1. Phil 1:12.

## Part Three: From Christ's Ascension to Christ's Return

There's no possible outcome that can extinguish Paul's joy, because "to live is Christ, and to die is gain."[2] This is an oft-repeated and seldom understood phrase, but the apostle's simply working out the implications of his union with Christ. To live is to walk in fellowship and communion with the Lord, tasting the blessings of his grace, following the way of the cross, sharing in his sufferings, and participating in his mission by faith. To die is to step into the presence of his King, to know by sight the one he's known by faith, and to experience an intimacy of fellowship with his Savior that at this point can hardly be imagined.

For the Christian, the move from this life to the next is a transition from one kind of joy—often tinged with the pangs of suffering—to another, one that's eternal and unbreakable. And though Paul recognizes that departing and being with Christ would be far better than anything he's ever experienced, he also sees that his continued ministry is necessary for the Philippians' joy and progress in the faith. So he resolves to come to them again in order to strengthen them with the truth and give them cause to glory in Christ. Many Christians in the midst of intense suffering have felt the longing to depart and be with Christ, but Paul shows us that our certain future with God, together with our present union with Christ and Jesus-exalting ministry of love to others, can be a powerful motive for joyful perseverance in this life.

In verse 27, Paul turns his attention to the Philippians and exhorts them to live in a manner worthy of the gospel of Christ. This doesn't mean, "Live in a way that shows you're worthy of God's grace." How ridiculous that would be! What he means is, "Live in a way that lines up with what God has done for you and who he's declared you to be in the gospel. Live out your heavenly citizenship here on earth." And he calls them to do this in two ways.

One way to live in line with the gospel is to exhibit grace-empowered courage in suffering and to not be frightened by the threats from opponents of the gospel. Jesus received the death we deserved at the cross and then overcame death in his resurrection. Christians can therefore stand courageously when confronted with marginalization, mockery, prison, and even death, knowing that even if we lose everything, we've lost nothing. But we can also take courage because the very God who gave us the gift of faith also grants us the privilege of suffering for the sake of Christ. God has appointed suffering for the gospel as part of our pilgrimage to his eternal kingdom,

2. Phil 1:21.

which means not only that our hardship is under his sovereign control, but also that he intends to magnify the worth and beauty of Jesus as we cling to him as our hope through the pain. So we can suffer in courage by faith in Jesus for the cause of Jesus to exalt the glory of Jesus.

In addition to this faithful fearlessness, Paul urges us to live in a manner worthy of the gospel by embodying the unity we have in Christ. Jesus has taken the many and made us one by his Spirit, and Christians embody this unity when we're single-minded in a sacrificial love toward one another that's fueled by the love we've received from the Father, the encouragement we have in Christ, and the fellowship we share in the Spirit. Especially during times of opposition and conflict that strain our already fragile relationships, this unity requires a dramatic humility. Selfishness and pride kill unity by pitting our desires against others' and spurring competitive rivalries, but humility fuels unity by counting others as more significant than ourselves and considering their interests above our own.

How is this kind of humble unity even possible? *We have to be humbled by the glorious humility of Christ.* The Son of God took on flesh. The King became a servant. The author of life submitted to a death of the most excruciating and humiliating variety. The one to whom all obedience is due obeyed in our place—all the way to the cross—in order to accomplish God's plan of redemption. Paul calls us to imitate Jesus because Jesus is the kind of God who not only commands humility, but who shows us how to walk in it: "Have this mind among yourselves."[3]

But he also says that this humble mind "is yours in Christ Jesus."[4] In other words, when you know Jesus as the Savior whose humility purchased your life—when you're united to Jesus by faith and you allow his gospel to re-narrate and reorient your entire life—you'll finally recognize the lengths that God went to in order to make you his own, and you'll begin to exhibit the humility of your Lord. The gospel not only proclaims the humility of Christ. It humbles you with a message of grace. Jesus is both the model and the motivation for the church's humility.

But Paul reminds us that after Christ's humiliation came exaltation. Because of his flawlessly humble obedience (notice that Paul uses the word "therefore" in verse 9), God vindicated and exalted his Son in the resurrection. The only one worthy of glory is in fact the one who refused to seek it, who instead walked the road of meekness and sacrifice as he exhibited

3. Phil 2:5.
4. Phil 2:5.

PART THREE: FROM CHRIST'S ASCENSION TO CHRIST'S RETURN

unyielding love toward God and the world. And on the last day, everyone—including the enemies of the gospel—will bow before Jesus either in glad adoration or in defeated rebellion.

Contemplating with Paul the exaltation of Christ, we find yet one more reason for joy as we anticipate life in the presence of our King, one more reason for courage as we look forward to his final victory over all the enemies of the gospel, and one more reason for humble unity as our proud confidence in ourselves is replaced by confidence together in our reigning Lord.

*Father, you've granted your people the privilege not only of believing in Christ, but also of suffering with him for the glory of his name. Preserve us in joy, grow us in courage, and humble us for unity so that we might persevere in the face of opposition and marginalization. Shape us by your Spirit with the promises of the cross and the hope of Jesus' exaltation so that we might live and speak faithfully in our life together and in our witness to the world.*

# 42

# A Pilgrim Faith

*Hebrews 11:1—12:2*

THE BOOK OF HEBREWS is basically an extended sermon about how Jesus completes the story of God. The author (we're not entirely sure who wrote it) repeatedly returns to the patterns, people, and promises of the Old Testament to demonstrate that Jesus is the glorious fulfillment of them all. But the book isn't just a lesson in how to understand the Bible. It's an exhortation to keep holding onto Jesus even when perseverance is costly.

Apparently, a community of Christians with Hebrew roots was experiencing oppression and feeling the temptation to revert back to an Old Testament form of Judaism in order to dodge the threat of persecution and make life easier. That's why the book of Hebrews focuses so emphatically on Jesus' relationship to the Old Testament. Why return to the shadow when God has given you the substance in Christ? Hebrews drives this message home: *Don't turn back. Stay faithful to the cross. Jesus is better.*

So Hebrews is a call to faith in the Christ who fulfills everything God's been doing in history. But what is faith? And how do we keep walking in it—how do we endure—when life is hard? That's the concern of this passage.

Hebrews 11:1 offers a working definition of faith: "Now faith is the assurance of things hoped for, the conviction of things not seen." Modern people often think of faith in opposition to reason, as if faith means sticking our heads in the sand, neglecting the life of the mind, and believing in ignorance without critical or careful thought. But the Bible doesn't pit faith against reason. Faith actually changes *how* we reason—trusting Christ frees us to finally reason rightly—by grounding us in God's story and shifting our fundamental loyalty to our Creator and Redeemer. In Scripture, faith is

## Part Three: From Christ's Ascension to Christ's Return

contrasted with *sight*. It takes God at his word and hopes with confidence *even when we can't see the reality he's told us is ours*. Faith trusts the promises God's made to us in Jesus—promises of forgiveness, of adoption, of a kingdom—during this age when we can only see these things with the eyes of our hearts.

Such faith has been the consistent mark of God's people throughout time. Old Testament saints received their commendation from God the exact same way New Testament believers do—by faith in his promises. Prior to the coming of Christ, God's people trusted his covenant word and were counted righteous as they looked forward to God's ultimate achievement of salvation. Now Christians look back to Jesus' life, death, and resurrection by faith, trusting that God's covenant promises are true in him. So while Christians on this side of the empty tomb have a greater clarity about God's purposes than the people of old ever did, the essence of faith as hope in God's promises remains the same.

The bulk of Hebrews 11 is devoted to cataloguing the faith of Old Testament believers. Abel, Noah, Abraham, Moses, and a host of others are held up as faithful examples that Christians can learn from and emulate. But there's a consistent theme running through the chapter that we can't afford to miss. All these saints trusted God in a way that empowered their endurance in the middle of disappointment, opposition, suffering, and death, though they couldn't see all the blessings God had promised. And the author of Hebrews wants Christians to persevere through hardship with the same kind of hope—a hope that rests assured in God's promises while they're yet unseen.

Hebrews 11 consistently portrays people of faith as *pilgrims*: "These all died in faith, not having received the things promised, but having seen them and greeted them from afar, and having acknowledged that they were strangers and exiles on the earth."[1] These Old Testament figures lived in a hostile world, refusing to put their hope in the kingdoms they could see, and instead counted God's kingdom as their home while they held on to the promise that it would one day be restored.

Just like the people of old, Christians are pilgrims. We're "sojourners and exiles"[2] on our way to the heavenly homeland, citizens of God's kingdom who still live among the kingdoms of the world in a creation marred by the curse of sin as we await Christ's renewing return. As pilgrims, we can

1. Heb 11:13.
2. 1 Pet 2:11.

therefore expect marginalization because our ultimate allegiance, priorities, ethics, rhythms of life, and character—shaped by God's kingdom—will always leave us, to one degree or another, outsiders in the cultures in which we live.

But our present hope that we're citizens in God's kingdom now and our future hope that the kingdom will arrive in full both empower our perseverance while we suffer as pilgrims. The saints of old "suffered mocking and flogging, and even chains and imprisonment. They were stoned, they were sawn in two, they were killed with the sword. They went about in skins of sheep and goats, destitute, afflicted, mistreated."[3] But they remained steadfast in the faith because they looked to the reward of life and fellowship with the God who was their treasure. Knowing the God of promise enabled them to count their sufferings as more precious than the praise and wealth of the world.

In the same way, Christians have to resist the allure of worldliness and the temptation of conformity by fixing our hope on the treasure we have in Jesus by faith, the treasure we'll have by sight when he completes his kingdom and our eyes behold our Lord. We can gladly accept the reproach of the world and joyfully embrace our outsider status, living as faithful pilgrims who persevere in holiness and hope because the kingdom Jesus inaugurated will be established soon.

Old Testament believers endured tribulation as they trusted God, but they never received what was promised. They didn't hear Jesus announce that the kingdom is near. They didn't behold the death that reconciled sinners to God. They didn't see his resurrection from the dead and his ascension as God's victorious King. But through the testimony of Scripture, *we have*. So even while we wait for the promise to come to completion, we know that in Christ the promise has been fulfilled.

Armed with this hope and surrounded by so many witnesses who modeled perseverance through hardship, Christians must "run with endurance the race that is set before us,"[4] laying aside the sin that ties our hearts to created comforts and standing firm in faith and faithfulness as God's kingdom people.

And how do we do that? By looking to Jesus. He's the "founder and perfecter of our faith,"[5] the object of our hope who accomplished God's

---

3. Heb 11:36–37.
4. Heb 12:1.
5. Heb 12:2.

## Part Three: From Christ's Ascension to Christ's Return

purposes in history. So we can know that God's promises will surely come to pass because they've received their "Yes" in Christ. Jesus endured the agony and shame of the cross as he looked forward to the joy of vindication from God and a kingdom in which to dwell with his redeemed people. So we can endure suffering in faith, looking ahead to the joy Jesus secured for us and trusting that the shame we receive from the world will melt away under the rays of God's pleasure. Jesus is "seated at the right hand of the throne of God."[6] He's the King right now, and he'll return as King to make all the hopes of God's people a glorious reality. So we can live with the confidence that the kingdom we're part of will one day fill the earth, that we'll one day see the God and the kingdom we've clung to by faith.

*Great God, you've given us precious kingdom promises, and in Christ you've kept them all. As we consider the faithful witness of the Old Testament saints, help us to persevere in the faith as pilgrims who are looking forward to the homeland Jesus purchased for us at the cross. Fix our hearts on your Son, who endured death for us so that we might endure even unto death for you.*

---

6. Heb 12:2.

# 43

# The Throne and the Lamb
## *Revelation 4–5*

WITH THIS MEDITATION, WE at last come to the final book of the Bible. Revelation is often approached with equal parts fascination and fear, stemming from the fact that it's uniquely saturated with intensely vivid and highly symbolic images that are sometimes quite difficult to understand. The first step toward appreciating Revelation's place in the story of the Bible is to recognize what kind of writing it is. This book is neither simply narrative (like the Gospels or Acts) nor epistle (like the New Testament letters), so we can't read it as a straightforward, chronological, and literal account the way we would other portions of Scripture. Rather, it's *apocalyptic* writing, which utilizes figurative and symbolic language—often drawn from the pages of the Old Testament—to offer a true and trustworthy heavenly perspective on history.

In chapters 4–5, John receives a vision of the throne room of heaven, where he sees God enthroned in glory and power. God is the King above every king who exercises sovereign control over all of creation and is therefore able to faithfully direct history to his appointed purposes. Recalling Ezekiel's vision of the Lord in Ezekiel 1, John likens God's beauty to the splendor of precious stones, and the rainbow encircling the throne evokes memories of God's saving grace toward Noah in the midst of his judgment against sin, as well as his promise to exercise merciful patience with his world. Even in his judgment of the world during the course of history—which Revelation describes in great detail—God's inviting the world to repentance, and he'll preserve his covenant people through it all just as he did Noah and his family.

# Part Three: From Christ's Ascension to Christ's Return

Surrounding God's throne are twenty-four thrones with twenty-four elders seated on them. The twenty-four elders (standing for the twelve tribes of Israel and the twelve apostles) together represent the whole community of God's people throughout the ages—both the Old Testament saints who looked ahead in faith to Christ's coming and the New Testament saints who look back in faith to the cross. In Daniel 7:9–10, Daniel saw thrones surrounding the Ancient of Days from which God's people were granted kingly authority. And that's precisely what John describes in Revelation as God's people are clothed in white garments and golden crowns as forgiven, royal children.

Before God's throne, the sea—the symbolic source of evil and chaos—is so still that it looks like a sea of glass. Though the devil rages against God's people, though evil wreaks havoc on the world, the point here is that, from God's perspective, they're completely under control. God's gracious sovereignty extends even over sin, death, and Satan, and in the death and resurrection of Jesus he secured their ultimate defeat. We're awaiting the day when Christ returns to do away with them entirely, but if we view history from the vantage point of God's throne, we find that God's kingship means that there's nothing to fear.

John also sees four living creatures around the throne, ceaselessly proclaiming God's holiness, power, and eternity. The (admittedly odd) descriptions of these figures suggest that they represent the entire created order. In so many places throughout the Bible, God tells us that he formed all of creation for his glory and that his creative works reveal his power and declare his praise,[1] and John's vision confirms these truths yet again.

And whenever the four living creatures break forth in worship, the twenty-four elders follow their lead. God's people, rescued from our sin and reconciled to our Father, have the privilege of accompanying the chorus of creation in humble and jubilant thanksgiving, adoration, and praise. The saints in heaven worship God in his presence, and the saints on earth are to join in as well, delighting in his glory. John lets us listen in to these heavenly hymns so that we'll lift our hearts in worship, because the Creator of all things, the sovereign Lord of glory, the King who lives forever and ever is ours, and we are his.

In God's right hand is a scroll with writing covering the front and back, sealed with seven seals. In the imagery of Revelation, this scroll represents God's comprehensive plan for history, including both his judgment of

---

1. For example, Ps 19:1–6; Rom 1:20.

sin and his redemption of his covenant people. But when no one is found in heaven or on earth who's worthy to open the scroll—that is, to bring God's purposes to completion—John weeps. If no one can open the scroll, God's purposes for history will go unfulfilled, and his people will be left without hope.

But John can wipe away his tears because the Lion of the tribe of Judah, the Root of David, has conquered and is worthy to execute God's plan. Genesis 49:9–10 promised that from the line of Judah a lion-like king would arise and receive the obedience of all peoples, and Isaiah 11 anticipated a shoot that would emerge from the seemingly dead stump of David's royal family. Jesus is the royal lion, the long awaited messianic King, who conquers the enemies of God's people and in so doing ensures that God's purposes are accomplished.

As John looks, however, he sees something quite unexpected. The conquering lion is a slain lamb. And this tells us something profound about the way Jesus secures victory for his people: he wins by dying. The King of kings is the Passover Lamb whose blood covers the sins of his people. The Lord of lords is the suffering servant who, "like a lamb that is led to the slaughter,"[2] bears the iniquities of sinners like us. Jesus conquered sin, death, and Satan by allowing them to seemingly conquer him, but when he gave his life away at the cross, he stripped them of their power over the church and demonstrated his victory through his resurrection from the dead.

When Jesus takes the scroll from God the Father, heaven erupts again in worship. Jesus can open the seals and bring God's plan of redemption to completion because at the cross he purchased with his blood a people from every tribe, language, people, and nation so that we might reign as priests and kings in the presence of God. When you truly grasp the magnitude of Jesus' accomplishments for you and for the world, the gospel will animate your worship, and you'll join the saints in heaven and all of creation in ascribing honor and glory to your King.

When John wrote the book of Revelation, the church was experiencing considerable oppression and persecution from the political and social powers of the Roman empire. And to varying degrees, this has been true of the church in every time and place as God's people cling in faith to a message that challenges the norms of every society. But John's vision in Revelation 4–5 is a source of great comfort and hopeful perseverance. God's in

---

2. Isa 53:7.

## Part Three: From Christ's Ascension to Christ's Return

control of history, even the church's suffering. He's the eternal King whose reign will never end, unlike the fading crowns of earthly power. And his purposes will be brought to completion in Christ, who already defeated evil at the cross and will return to finish what he started.

*Our loving Father, you made everything, you hold it together, and you're sovereign over all of history. No king can compare, so we say, "Holy, holy, holy is the Lord God Almighty, who was and is and is to come!" You sent Jesus into the world as the lion who would conquer by becoming a lamb, and because of his death and resurrection your plans for redemption will certainly come to pass. He has prevailed over all our enemies, so we sing, "Worthy is the Lamb who was slain, to receive power and wealth and wisdom and might and honor and glory and blessing!"*

# 44

# The Thousand Years
## *Revelation 20*

REVELATION 20 MAY BE the most debated passage of the most debated book in the whole Bible. Godly, faithful Christians have disagreed over the precise meaning of this chapter throughout history. But we should nevertheless do our best to understand what God's saying to us here with as much clarity and conviction as possible—with ears attuned to the echoes of earlier parts of Scripture—as we consider how these verses contribute to the larger story of redemption that God is telling.

John's vision begins with the binding of Satan. This is a figurative way of saying that God has limited the devil's power "so that he might not deceive the nations any longer."[1] Satan, "that ancient serpent,"[2] deceived Adam and Eve in the garden in an effort to destroy the community of God's people. And throughout Israel's history, the devil worked among the nations to keep them from submitting to the Lord, threatening God's covenant nation with oppression and destruction.

But with Christ's death and resurrection, and with his sending of the Holy Spirit to empower the church for witness in the world, Satan's power to deceive the nations and destroy the church has taken a decisive hit. Jesus died and rose again to purchase a people from every tribe and tongue, and the Spirit will bring sinners from every nation to faith as he fuels the church's gospel proclamation and mission. And while Satan continues to prowl, lie, accuse, and even incite the world to violence against God's

---

1. Rev 20:3.
2. Rev 20:2.

people, he cannot threaten the spiritual life that believers have in Jesus, and he cannot ultimately destroy the covenant community that God promises to preserve.

Satan's binding lasts for a thousand years, a symbolic number that represents the entire church age from Christ's resurrection until his second coming. And during this same time period, John sees faithful believers who've died in the Lord alive and reigning with Jesus. Martyrs who lost their lives for the sake of the gospel and Christians who persevered in the faith—refusing to worship and trust the idols of the world—rule with Jesus in heaven as they await the resurrection of their bodies and the consummation of Christ's kingdom in the new heavens and new earth.

While these Christians who are (as the Apostle Paul might say) absent from the body and present with the Lord[3] have experienced physical death, they'll never be touched by spiritual death. The spiritual life that began with their regeneration and union with Christ will continue on forever. And just as Adam and Eve lived as kings and priests of God in Eden, so all who've died in the Lord will exercise royal authority with Christ and serve God in priestly worship. As 2 Timothy 2:11–12 promises, "If we have died with him, we will also live with him; if we endure, we will also reign with him."

During the era of the Spirit-empowered church, Satan's power is restricted, and God's people who've died live spiritually with their Lord. But John foresees a short time near the end when Satan will be loosed to deceive the nations and lead them in an effort to wipe out the covenant community. With symbolic language drawn heavily from Ezekiel 38–39, John anticipates that the world will be climactically unified in opposition against God's people, seemingly threatening their very existence.

But God ever lives with his people, and he'll act on their behalf, interceding with judgment against all who would harm the children he gave his life to protect. In Revelation the devil, the beast, and the false prophet act as an unholy, counterfeit Trinity and represent all the spiritual, political, and religious forces, people, and institutions that rage against God and his church. But the Lord who delivered his people from sin at the cross will deliver his people once and for all when he returns to exercise perfect justice against every form of rebellion and eternally judges everything that defames his glory, destroys his creation, and hurts the church he loves.

With verse 11, John shifts the scene from God's deliverance of his covenant people on earth to his final judgment of all humanity in heaven.

3. See 2 Cor 5:6–8.

## The Thousand Years

Both of these are perspectives on Christ's second coming as creation's king and judge. All the dead—believers and non-believers alike—will stand before the throne, the books of history will be opened, and everyone will be judged according to what they've done.

This would spell certain disaster for us all, except that another book is opened—the book of life, the citizenship registry of heaven that lists all those who've trusted in Jesus' provision for sin in the gospel. Everyone whose name isn't recorded in the book of life will receive God's wrath against their sin, but those who've been united to Christ by faith will receive God's mercy in spite of their sin. Far from leading to our condemnation, the (albeit imperfect) works of Christians—the lives born from repentance and faith—will serve as evidence of our hope in Christ and will be rewarded with God's pleasure and with stewardship in his kingdom.

Modern people in particular have a hard time accepting what the Bible has to say about judgment, wrath, and hell. It's often asked, *How could a loving God send people to hell?* But the story of the word shows us that God's holiness and justice aren't opposed to his goodness and love. They're intimately connected.

Love always drives us to protect and defend the one we love. Each person of the Trinity loves the others too completely to allow God's glory to be trampled without consequence. The Lord loves his world too fully to allow wickedness and rebellion to perpetually destroy his creation. And God loves his children—purchased at the cost of his only Son—too comprehensively to permit sin to threaten them forever. God's holy and righteous justice is one outworking of his loving commitment to himself, his world, and his church.

Revelation 20 offers us a highly symbolic perspective on the life of the church from Christ's resurrection to his return in glory, but John has a deeply practical reason for giving us this passage. Like the book of Revelation as a whole, this chapter is a call to persevere in hope and holiness and mission, a call to fight fear with the promises that God is sovereign, that God is gracious, that the Christian's death is an entrance into life, and that the victory Jesus secured at the cross will one day be brought to completion when evil is judged and death is destroyed.

Though Satan is at work in the world, the finished work of the cross and the presence of the Spirit ensure that the gospel will go forward in power and that God's people are secure, even in the midst of incredible oppression. And though Satan will roar when God releases him for a little

## Part Three: From Christ's Ascension to Christ's Return

while, he will roar as one dying, because his defeat is sure and certain and coming soon.

*Holy and loving Father, we thank you for your sovereign control over all of history—even the parts that hurt—and for your word that reveals your purposes to us. We thank you that Christ's death and resurrection for us mean that, even in death, we'll have life as kings and priests with our Lord Jesus. Guard our hearts from fear, preserve us in the faith, and strengthen us with confidence for mission with the promise that you're with us, that you're for us, and that you'll bring total justice and restoration to your world.*

# 45

# The End of All Things
*Revelation 21:1–8; 22:1–5*

WHAT YOU BELIEVE ABOUT the future will inevitably shape the way you live in the present. Or to put it another way, no matter what story you think you're part of, the ending of that story will determine how you play your part now. With Revelation 21–22, God's story of the world draws to a close. So many of the themes and promises that have been introduced, explored, and expanded throughout the Bible are here tied together, resolved, and gloriously fulfilled. And because God's people have seen the last page, because God has given us a glimpse of what our future holds, we can live today and always in hope, joy, faithful perseverance, and anticipation of a forever with God.

John's vision in chapter 21 begins with a new heaven and a new earth—an entirely restored cosmos—where the sea is no more. Throughout the Old Testament and in the book of Revelation, the sea functions symbolically as the place of chaos, evil, rebellion, and death. But in God's new world, all the corruption of sin, death, and Satan that began with the fall and have plagued the whole universe ever since will be eliminated entirely. Creation's groaning will finally be answered as God's people and God's world are resurrected in glory. The Bible's vision of heaven isn't one of disembodied spirits in the clouds, but physical bodies in a physical world that's saturated with the joy of the Lord.

Coming down out of heaven from God is the holy city, the new Jerusalem. But the holy city isn't just a place. It's a people, a bride adorned for her husband. The church—the covenant people of God—that was chosen for Jesus before time and purchased by Jesus at the cross in time is now presented to Jesus in splendor to live in the intimacy of covenant fellowship for all time. Just as God presented Eve to Adam in the first wedding ceremony, so now the Father walks the church down the aisle to Jesus her bridegroom in the marriage celebration to which every other marriage points.

A loud voice bursts forth from the throne declaring, "Behold, the dwelling place of God is with man. He will dwell with them, and they will be his people, and God himself will be with them as their God."[1] The promise of God's presence—given first to Abraham, prefigured in the temple, and embodied in the incarnation of Jesus Christ—now becomes a blessed reality for all those whose sins have been dealt with at the cross. The joyful communion that was forfeited in Eden is finally restored in full as God makes his home in the new creation among the people he created and rescued for himself.

And God's presence is a healing presence, a presence that drives out all the hurt and sadness that sin introduced into the world: "He will wipe away every tear from their eyes, and death shall be no more, neither shall there be mourning, nor crying, nor pain anymore, for the former things have passed away."[2] The prophet Isaiah looked ahead to a day when God would lay out a feast for all peoples and do away with death for good. "He will swallow up death forever; and the Lord God will wipe away tears from all faces, and the reproach of his people he will take away from all the earth."[3] At the cross, Jesus swallowed up death by allowing death to swallow him, and in the new heaven and new earth, God will throw away death forever and welcome us into the comfort and healing of never-ending life with him.

"It is finished!" was Christ's cry atop Golgotha when by his death he secured salvation for his people. Now John hears a similar declaration—"It is done!"[4]—as all the blessings Jesus died to purchase are poured out on the world. The Alpha and Omega—the God who's the originator, sovereign governor, and goal of all history—grants the water of life without payment. The only requirement is that we come thirsty, recognizing our need for Christ's saving grace. This inheritance—life with God in a totally restored creation—is given to everyone who conquers by holding fast to the gospel during this present, trial-filled age.[5]

1. Rev 21:3.
2. Rev 21:4.
3. Isa 25:8.
4. Rev 21:6.
5. See 1 John 2:4–5; Rev 2:26; 12:11.

God says to the thirsty, conquering believer, "I will be his God, and he will be my son,"[6] echoing his covenant with King David. There the Lord promised a royal heir and swore, "I will be to him a father, and he shall be to me a son."[7] Jesus of course is the final fulfillment of this covenant, the resurrected and ascended King who eternally rules over God's kingdom. But Jesus shares with everyone who's united to him by faith the privilege of reigning as kings over his new world. Jesus is the royal Son of the Father, and in him, every Christian is a royal son, too. Those who unrepentantly cling to their sin, however, will receive not God's presence and blessing, but his wrath, as their portion.

In Ezekiel 47, the prophet described his vision of the restored temple of God. A teeming river flowed from this temple, and on both its banks trees blossomed with fruit that never failed and leaves that offered healing. These same images are used to describe God's heavenly city in Revelation 22. Why? Because the city of God is the temple of God. The whole earth is the place where the Lord dwells in glory with his people.

And as God's temple-city, the new Jerusalem is the restoration and completion of all that was lost in Eden. The tree of life from which Adam and Eve were barred now stands in the city of God, never going out of season, conferring life and healing to the nations. Because Jesus gave up his life on the tree of death, God's promise to Abraham of blessing for all peoples becomes a visible reality. In this city, nothing is accursed, because Christ bore the curse so that God's gracious blessing could cover the cosmos. And God's children, marked out with God's name, will worship him in the splendor of his holiness, see his face with their very own eyes, and reign with Jesus forever and ever.

The story of the Bible began in a garden where God dwelt with image bearers who were called to imitate his kingship in worship and obedience. And the story ends in a bountiful city where God resides eternally with a new humanity—perfectly conformed to the image of Christ—who live as his royal children in never-ending joy and never-ceasing praise.

But in one sense, this ending is only another glorious beginning. At the end of *The Last Battle*, the final book of *The Chronicles of Narnia*, C. S. Lewis writes,

> And for us this is the end of all the stories, and we can most truly say that they all lived happily ever after. But for them it was only

---

6. Rev 21:7.

7. 2 Sam 7:14.

the beginning of the real story. All their life in this world and all their adventures in Narnia had only been the cover and the title page: now at last they were beginning Chapter One of the Great Story which no one on earth has read: which goes on forever: in which every chapter is better than the one before.[8]

In the same way, the conclusion of the Bible is but the start of an eternity in the presence of the Lord, where we'll keep on living and worshiping and serving and cultivating and singing and playing and exploring the depths of God's beautiful character and works forever and for always.

And so we say, "Come, Lord Jesus!"[9]

*God and Father of our Lord Jesus Christ, we praise you now in the hope that we'll behold your glory in worship forever. Thank you for the promise that you'll make all things new, wipe away every tear, and bring perfect justice, righteousness, and peace to your world. Give us hearts that long for the return of Jesus and the renewal of all creation. And as you plant the story of your word deep in our hearts by your Holy Spirit, help us to live into your story as faithful children who love, trust, and obey you in every aspect of our lives. Come quickly, Lord Jesus! Amen.*

---

8. C. S. Lewis, *The Last Battle* (New York: Scholastic, 1956), 210–11.
9. Rev 22:20.

www.ingramcontent.com/pod-product-compliance
Lightning Source LLC
Chambersburg PA
CBHW051055160426
43193CB00010B/1193